THE CRAFT
OF WOOD CARVING

THE CRAFT OF
Wood
CARVING

Alan & Gill Bridgewater

David & Charles
Newton Abbot London

To Mrs G. Williamson
In Loving Memory

British Library Cataloguing in Publication Data

Bridgewater, Alan
  The craft of wood carving.
  1. Wood-carving – Technique
  I. Title II. Bridgewater, Gill
  731.4'62   NK9704

  ISBN 0–7153–8035–4

Typeset and printed in Great Britain
by Redwood Burn Limited, Trowbridge
for David & Charles (Publishers) Limited
Brunel House   Newton Abbot   Devon

CONTENTS

INTRODUCTION   7

1   **TOOLS, WOOD AND PATTERNS**   9
Caring for tools – making a bench – types of wood – techniques used world-
wide – how to prepare wood and lay out the patterns

2   **CHIP CARVING, ADZE AND KNIFE WORK**   35
Suitable tools and wood – step-by-step carving of one specific design – ethnic,
primitive and basic carving – American, African and European tribal carving

3   **FLAT CHISEL AND ROUND GOUGE WORK**   58
Medieval carving – misericords – step-by-step carving of one design

4   **BUILT-UP, DRILLED AND PIERCED WORK**   82
Grinling Gibbons – eighteenth century furniture makers – step-by-step instructions for a grille or room-divider screen

5   **TURNED WORK, FURNITURE AND DOMESTIC WARE**   105
Lathes – stately home furniture – cottage chairs – step-by-step instructions for a
turned container and Welsh milking stool – treen – making a letter-knife love
token

6   **INLAY, MARQUETRY AND TUNBRIDGE WARE**   128
History – instructions for an inlay design on existing furniture – marquetry chess
board, turned and whittled chessmen – marquetry veneers list – instructions for
a Tunbridge ware pattern

CONCLUSION   147
Design Appreciation, Texture, Form and Drawing

GLOSSARY OF TOOLS   150

BIBLIOGRAPHY   153

ACKNOWLEDGEMENTS   154

INDEX   155

INTRODUCTION

World travel, television and other improved communications have rekindled in artists, craftsmen and hobbyists an awareness of the rightness of natural materials. We in the West, inspired by ethnic art forms, are trying to rediscover our own craft heritage. This book is for both the serious wood carver and the struggling adult beginner. It not only gives step-by-step guides to specific wood carving techniques, but also places the carvings in a historical, geographical and chronological context.

Wood is a readily available material which can be found in most parts of the world, so we can not only relate our wood carving to that made in Europe and the West, but also to that made in more basic and perhaps unfamiliar ethnic communities.

The story of Western and European carving is to a great extent the story of many generations of simple and uncomplicated workmen. Using home-made and very basic tools, these humble craftsmen shaped our homes, our churches and a whole myriad of everyday objects. The earliest work found in Europe is recognised by the honest approach to materials and form – this directness in wood carving is often captured in naive and humorous design subjects. The twined beasts on ancient Scandinavian buildings, the powerful patterns on early European chests and tables and the romantic and often very earthy design themes on medieval misericords and pew-ends – they all bear witness to a flourishing wood carving tradition.

The marks on the wood left by the knife, the adze and the gouge are all-important, and 'finish' as used in the modern sense must not be allowed to govern our understanding of the craft. The furniture and interior carvers of the seventeenth and eighteenth centuries gradually became so obsessed with what they considered 'style', good taste and finish that they eventually emasculated their craft roots. Now that carved wood is again being used by architects, furniture designers and artists, there is a growing interest in the beautiful and forgotten carvings that are hidden away in our stately homes, churches and museums.

As well as looking and relating to our own wood carving past, we must try to learn and understand more about the tools, patterns and traditions of the tribal and primitive carvings of America, Africa and Oceania.

In writing this book we are not only attempting to give practical guidance to the student and beginner, but showing that a broader understanding of world-wide design is an essential part of good craftsmanship. In the recent past misguided craftsmen have mechanically applied 'ornamentation' without any consideration of the materials, but with the new resurgence of interest in all the crafts, it can clearly be seen that materials, workmanship, and design are inseparable. The carvers of medieval England, and the tribal carvers of America and Africa worked with their tools and materials, not against them. We cannot regain a lost innocence, but we can look to the craftsmen of the past and the ethnic carvers of the present and benefit from what we see of their deep understanding of the materials.

1   In this 15th century altar painting St Joseph
the carpenter is shown using typical wood
working tools of the medieval period. Tools of
similar design were in common use right up until
the end of the 19th century – in my own workshop
I have a chisel which is almost identical to the fish
tail chisel that is shown on St Joseph's bench.

1

TOOLS, WOOD AND PATTERNS

Tools

There are quite literally thousands of wood carving tools – planes, chisels, gouges, knives, drills, draw planes, hatchets, axes, adzes, scrapers, saws, files – the list is endless. For the beginner it is best to get as few tools as possible and build on this basic collection.

MALLETS

You will need a wooden carver's mallet. This can either be a round heavy cylindrical traditional mallet made of a dense wood such as lignum vitae, or it can be a convenient lump of shaped timber offcut. Whichever you choose, it must be heavy enough to do the work for you, but not so heavy that you cannot lift your arm.

CHISELS AND GOUGES

Many of the chisel and gouge types have evolved with usage; individual craftsmen would order the blacksmith to make tools that had precise shapes. These individual tools fitted the requirements of particular carvers. But for the beginner I would suggest that half a dozen chisels or gouges would be adequate, say a couple of straight chisels, a couple of straight gouges and two or three curved gouges. As you progress with your carving you will eventually require specific tools for particular tasks.

RASPS, FILES AND ABRADING TOOLS

There are now many patented rasp-type tools on the market. They have the added advantage that as they cut, the wood passes through the 'grater' cutters so they do not readily clog up. These tools are so efficient that they must be used with caution.

Forming tools now come in a variety of shapes and sizes, but basically there are three main types – the flat 'plane' model which is held in both hands, the single-handed small shaper and the long narrow tube 'hole' shaper. Tools of this type are uncomplicated; they are used like a file or a plane, and when the blade loses its edge or gets damaged it is unscrewed from the metal or plastic frame and replaced.

When a rasp has been used the wood will be left with a ridged or furrowed surface. If you require a finer finish there are several other tools that you could use. The riffler is a small usually spoon-shaped rasp, just the tool to use for those awkward and difficult

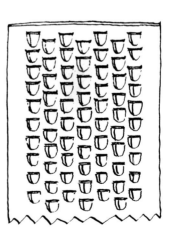

2   Many of the modern open tooth rasps and shaping tools are so designed that the cutting edges are self clearing; this increase in efficiency means that they have to be used with considerable caution.

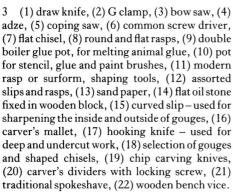

3   (1) draw knife, (2) G clamp, (3) bow saw, (4) adze, (5) coping saw, (6) common screw driver, (7) flat chisel, (8) round and flat rasps, (9) double boiler glue pot, for melting animal glue, (10) pot for stencil, glue and paint brushes, (11) modern rasp or surform, shaping tools, (12) assorted slips and rasps, (13) sand paper, (14) flat oil stone fixed in wooden block, (15) curved slip – used for sharpening the inside and outside of gouges, (16) carver's mallet, (17) hooking knife – used for deep and undercut work, (18) selection of gouges and shaped chisels, (19) chip carving knives, (20) carver's dividers with locking screw, (21) traditional spokeshave, (22) wooden bench vice.

4   There are so many chisels and gouges on the market, that the student wood carver is often overwhelmed and confused. If you have the chance of obtaining second hand tools then you will be at a great advantage, as years of constant care and usage will almost certainly have worn them to keen perfection. These particular tools belong to a man whose family has been carving over many generations. Jack Hazelwood, the latest in the line, is using tools which are perhaps two or three hundred years old.

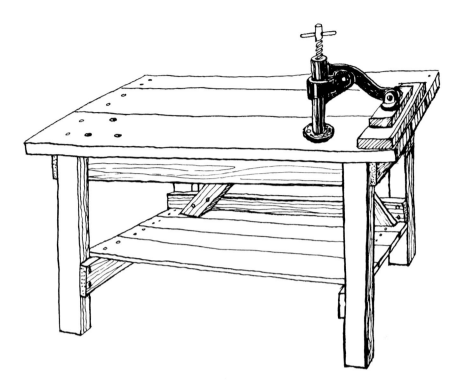

corners. If you require a fine smooth effect, a metal or glass scraper dragged across the surface of the wood will give a good finish. Finally the wood can be smoothed with graded sandpapers.

Apart from these basic wood carving tools you will need a straight-forward selection of carpenter's tools. Saws, drills, planes, draw planes – sooner or later you will find a use for them all.

BENCH AND HOLDING METHODS
Every wood carver will need a bench or work surface. You could make do with a large wooden farmhouse-type kitchen table, but as these are becoming more difficult to obtain it would perhaps be best to build a bench of your own. Ideally the top should be made of boards at least 6 cm thick and the total vertical height should be 100–120 cm. The bench needs to be steady and as large as workshop space allows.

There are several methods of holding the wood secure while you carve, the choice relating to the size and shape of your particular piece of wood. A large stout engineer's vice with a swivel movement is perfect for bulky

5   Every carver will need a bench – they are easy to make and should be as large as space allows. This particular one is about 100–120 cm in total height and constructed with top boards that are at least 6 cm thick. The type of holdfast illustrated is most suited for securing large irregular lumps of wood and is a very flexible piece of equipment.

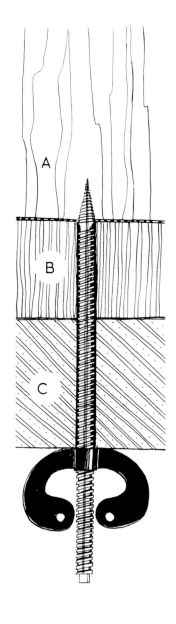

6 If you are carving a large work that needs all-round attention, then the bench screw is the best holding method to use. First a piece of scrap wood is attached and glued to the base of your work – then the bench screw is screwed into it. The work plus screw is then placed on your bench so that the screw passes through a hole in the bench surface and the whole thing is secured underneath with a large wing nut.

(A) Work
(B) Scrapwood
(C) Bench

7 Tools need to be very sharp – I should say that on average more time is spent sharpening tools than using them, so you may as well do it correctly.
(A) The bevel of this flat chisel is sharpened to an angle of between 5°–10°, the rule is – the harder the wood, the smaller the angle.
(B) With the corner chisel, both sides are bevelled, also the corner is rubbed off, this ensures that inside corner cuts are sharp and clean.
(C) With the deep gouge, the outer bevel is brought to an angle of about 10° and the inner blade edge is just touched with the sharpening slip.
(D) Parting tools usually have a 10° outer bevel, on no account should the outer angle be ground and rounded.
(E) There are many types of adzes, but this particular one is sharpened to an angle of 5°–10° on the inner edge.
(F) Chip carving tools can be sharpened as you like, but I personally prefer an angle of about 12°.

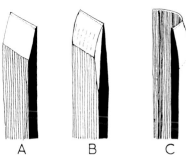

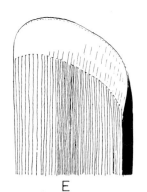

A   B   C   D   E   F

8 The round gouge is best sharpened in a curved 'figure 8' pattern but it must at the same time be rocked gently from side to side. For a really keen edge, it must also be stropped on a piece of thick oiled leather.

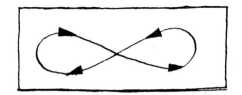

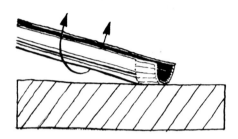

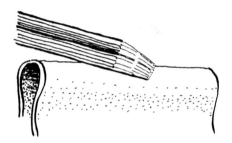

9 As the gouges are sharpened in the 'figure 8' pattern, your wrist must be rocked from side to side – this isn't easy and it will need considerable practice.

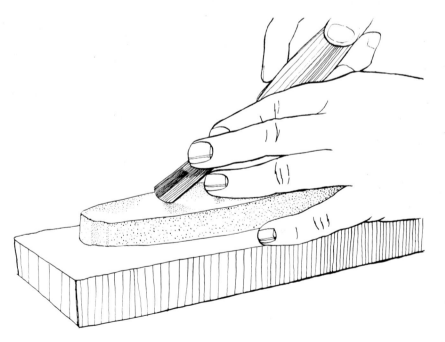

irregular work. The metal removable jaws can be unscrewed and replaced with hardwood blocks – this prevents tearing and damage to the surface of the wood. Small flat panels can be secured with G clamps or holdfasts. All these appliances have their advantages and limitations. If you are carving a large heavy block you could do worse than bedding it in a sack full of old rags or foam scrap.

CARING FOR TOOLS

If your tools are blunt and chipped you may as well give up; there is nothing so discouraging as trying to make a clean cut and finishing up with a splintered tear.

SHARPENING TOOLS

You will need a grindstone, oilstones and slips. A grindstone is a power – or foot–driven disc which revolves at low speeds through a trough of water. This is used when the cutting tools are in a bad condition and have to be reground. The water, as well as keeping down the dust, ensures that the tools are kept cool. You must not attempt to grind the tools at high speed on a dry wheel; if you do, the heat will take the temper out of

the steel and the tool will be ruined.

Flat chisels and the outer bevels of gouges can be sharpened on flat blocks of natural or artificial oilstone. They come in all shapes, sizes, grades and names, but all you really need are a coarse, a medium and a fine. The oilstone can either be fixed permanently in a wooden box on the bench, or it can be positioned against a bench stop. Before you sharpen your tools it is necessary to know whether you are going to use a hard or soft wood. This decision governs the angle at which the tools are sharpened. The rule is – a long fine-angled bevel for hard wood, and a short large-angled bevel for soft wood. Place the chisel on the stone at an angle of about 15° with the handle in the right hand and the fingers of the left hand pressing down on the shaft. With the stone well oiled, rub the chisel backwards and forwards along the stone keeping the chisel at the same angle and trying not to rock the handle.

The gouge is sharpened at the same angle as the chisel, but as well as moving the blade

10 The shaped slips must be stroked through the inside and outside edges of gouges – only sharpen on the downward stroke.

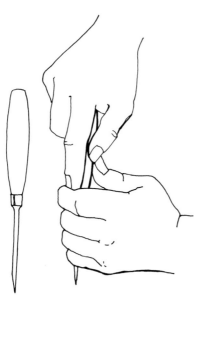

backwards and forwards on the oilstone, the gouge is gently rolled from side to side. The gouge is moved in a figure of eight, and rolled at the same time. This motion is tricky and will have to be practised, but your aim must be to get an even cutting edge.

When the outside edge of the blade has been sharpened on the flat oilstone, you use the slip to sharpen the inside edge. The slips are shaped oilstones which are used in a series of short strokes, down, through and across the hollow of the gouge. Finally, to remove all the burrs from the edge of the tool, the blade has to be rubbed or stropped on a piece of thick leather. If you want a really keen edge, a mixture of crocus powder

(*above left*)
11   When you are 'cutting in' your designs, the chisel is pushed into the wood with your right hand and guided and supported with the left – it is important that both hands are used, otherwise there is a danger of the chisel slipping or going out of control.

(*below left*)
12   A front-bent, round-edge gouge of this pattern would be used for removing small amounts of wood – it is a fine tool and should on no account be levered or twisted.

(*opposite page*)
(*above left*)
13   There is no point in chiselling away large areas of unwanted wood; it is much easier to use a saw. There are some really good coping saws on the market; they come in all shapes and sizes and have the added advantage of flexible, easily replaced blades.

(*above right*)
14   With your work held firmly in the vice or carver's chops, the large areas of unwanted wood can be sawn away – the mallet and chisel are used to rough out large areas. Always cut away from your body, and never cut directly into the grain of the wood.

(*below left*)
15   If you need to cut a shallow depression, this is best done with a gouge. Obviously each piece of work has to be approached differently, but try wherever possible to cut across the grain.

(*below right*)
16   If you want your work to have a fine un-tooled finish, then you can use either a rasp, or a surform-type, cutting plane, and finally the wood can be rubbed with graded sandpapers.

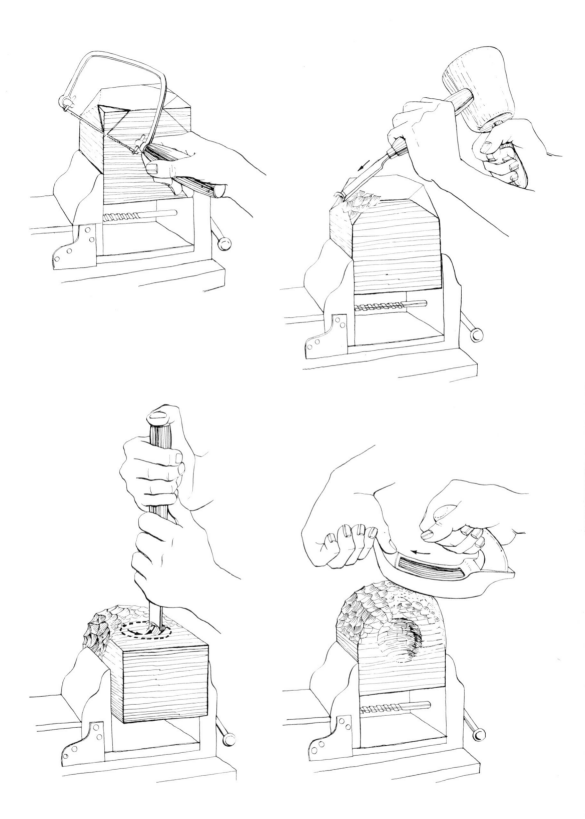

(opposite)

17 This detail from an Art Nouveau panel illustrates beautifully the use of careful tooling; it is rather 'self conscious' in style, but the marks left by the tools are used to great effect (*Rutland County Museum*).

and grease is rubbed on the strop and the blade given a final rub.

Once the tools have been sharpened they are ready for use and in use they will need to be stropped and oilstoned occasionally just to keep them in peak condition. All the chisels and gouges will have to be sharpened as I have described; the basic method will always be the same though of course each tool will have to be treated in a slightly different way according to its size and shape.

USING THE TOOLS

In almost all cases the wood to be worked is fixed, clamped or gripped firmly to the bench so that you have both your hands free. As you need to be totally in control of the cutting tools, they must always be held or manoeuvred with both hands, and you must always work away from your body. The chisels and gouges are held in the right hand and guided with the left. The right hand does the pushing and supplies the force, while the left hand guides, breaks and controls the movements of the right hand. I am at the moment describing how to hand-carve using only the driving force of the right hand, but if you want to remove large amounts of wood then you hold the cutting tool in the left hand and strike it with the mallet which is held in the right hand.

18 (A) The outer bark. (B) Phloem – or the outer cells of the new growth, gradually help to build up the bark layer of the tree. (C) Cambium are the thin cells that eventually increase the total girth of the tree. (D) Once the Cambium cells have developed they start to divide – the outer portions become the Phloem or bark, and the inner ones carry on developing and finally become Xylem, or the new wood.

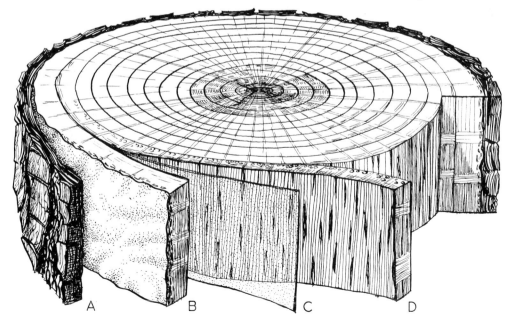

A   B   C   D

It must always be remembered that wood is not an even-textured material like soap or plastic. It has a grain and direction which dictates how it should be carved. As a general rule it is easier to cut across the grain than with it, so if you have to remove a lot of wood then you would be advised to work across the grain. When you have to rough out a large work, do not attempt to drive the gouge into the wood and then lever – all you will succeed in doing is splitting the wood and/or bending the tool. It is much better to remove small shallow scallops of wood at speed and always be prepared for the unexpected twist or knot in the grain.

Types of Wood

Wood is not manufactured – it grows. Trees mature and develop through bad winters – good winters – springs – dry summers – wet

19 The star shakes on the end of this log are caused by rapid drying; this type of fault is not as serious as heart shakes, but if possible the wood should be avoided.

summers: each tree is made and moulded by its changing yearly environment. Each year's growth is gradually covered by the successive growth of following years. When a tree is cut down the cross-sectional rings are records of yearly progress and development. The small rings in the centre of the trunk were once the seedling tree. The first few years of growth can hardly be seen with the naked eye, but gradually after the first seven or eight years the annual rings can be counted. At one time or other every part of the tree started off life as sapwood, and as it gets older, it in a sense 'retires' and becomes heartwood. The heartwood cells no longer used for carrying foods gradually become filled with resins and gums – it is these substances which give the heartwood its characteristic weight and dark colour. This heartwood, which no longer plays an active part in the growth of the tree, supports, reinforces and gives strength to the tree structure. The strength of any one tree is related to where it was grown and the seasons through which it has grown, but that apart, trees are described as being 'hard' or 'soft'. This description doesn't mean that hard woods are always harder than soft woods; it is more a generalisation which describes the overall qualities of particular woods. So for example by hard we mean that in use the wood is less likely to be damaged by impact than soft wood.

PROBLEMS WITH WOOD

As with all forms of growth, whether it be animal or plant, trees are subject to diseases, defects and flaws. It is important that as a worker in wood you are able to decide whether the defect is structural or superficial.

SHAKES

Shakes are separations and breaks which occur in annual growth rings and vertical faults which occur up through the tree structure. Shakes can be serious in certain instances as they are sometimes hidden and difficult to detect. From a carver's point of view, 'star' shakes that can be seen on the outside of a piece of timber are indications that the wood was kiln-dried too quickly –

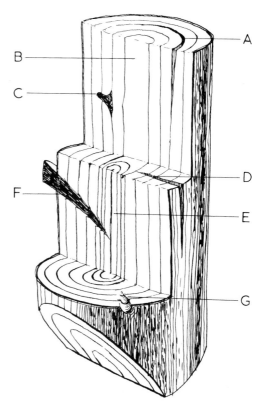

20 (A) Round or cup shakes. (B) Off-centre vertical cuts result in uneven grain spacing. (C) Faults, such as old bits of bark which remain hidden deep within the tree, always present the carver with unforseen difficulties. (D) Medular splits which go through to the heartwood are caused by sudden drying – timber with this fault should if possible be avoided. (E) Heartwood. (F) Knot caused by the 'root' of a branch – a serious fault. (G) A hole left by a dead knot.

don't worry too much about it, but if possible avoid any end timber where this defect is obvious. 'Heart' shakes are vertical breaks in the centre of the heartwood, they are usually the result of shrinkage and old age. When you buy a piece of wood always have a good look at the end section, but as this defect occurs in the centre of the wood and radiates out from the pith it is usually difficult to spot.

KNOTS AND HOLES

There are 'sound' knots, 'tight' knots, 'loose' knots and many others. Their names are descriptive of the problems they present. For example the 'loose' knot is liable to drop out, leaving a great hole in your work; this might be an advantage if you are carving a large abstracted sculptural form, but as a rule 'knot' wood is to be avoided. One way of finding out if a piece of wood has any holes, knots or shakes is to give it a tap with a mallet and compare the sound with that made on known good timber of the same variety.

WOOD GRAIN AND FIGURE PATTERNS

Carvers love and curse grain and figure patterns – they leave marks on the finished carvings which are as personal, unique and individual as fingerprints, so they must always be considered. The annual rings are alternately dark and light. Spring growth is marked by the light rings and summer growth by the dark rings. As a generalisation the growth rings tend to be less marked in hard woods. When the wood is sawn or cut the annual rings become more or less apparent. A cut straight across a tree reveals the annual rings as circles, but if the tree is cut at a sharp angle the annual rings appear as elipses. If a section is cut through a tree, and this section split off-centre vertically, the annual rings appear as vertical lines which are close together at the outside of the wood and wide apart at the centre. It soon becomes obvious that the pattern or grain of the cut wood is relative to how it was cut from the tree, and the type of tree.

As trees are always curved and have branches, it stands to reason that each and every piece of cut wood has well-defined individual characteristics, which enable you to tell exactly how it was cut, whereabouts in the tree it grew and whether the tree was tall, thin and straight like a pine, or a short, broad, many-branched tree like an oak. In certain trees when a section is taken from the trunk, there are distinctive marks which radiate out from the pith centre: these are known as medullary rays. In some types of wood medullary rays are very marked, so that as well as an annual ring pattern, the wood has marks which are the result of cuts through the rays.

Woods can be described as 'hard', 'soft', 'straight-grained', 'close-grained', 'coarse-grained', etc. How your wood appears when it is converted into timber depends wholly on the way it is sawn at the mill. There are timber merchants who specialise in wood for wood workers and carvers and it is to these people that you should go for your materials.

WOOD SEASONING

A growing tree is at least 50 per cent water. If it were cut and immediately used, it would so shrink and move that it would probably pull itself apart. Cells in a living tree grow at different rates, so when the tree is cut down they shrink at different rates – there is a tremendous variation in the time taken for different parts of the tree to dry out. Ideally when the tree has been converted into timber it should be stacked and dried in the open air; this in the past has been a lengthy business, taking anything up to ten years. Most of the timber that we now use is kiln-dried – this usually takes about two or three weeks. For traditional repeat pattern carving it would be best if you only used well-seasoned and suitably patterned timber. If you intend to carve abstracted sculptural forms you could perhaps collect free wood in rural areas – trees are always falling or being cut down, and in the towns good wood can be bought from demolition sites. Point – always be on the look-out for nails and bits of iron in old timber; they are often buried deep within the wood and they can make a real mess of a saw or chisel.

Soft Woods

CANADIAN RED CEDAR
This tree grows to a great size. It is easy to work and free from knots. It is good for interior as well as exterior usage and is best waxed – the finish will be fine and silky.

DOUGLAS FIR
This is called by a variety of names – Columbian pine, red pine, red fir, yellow fir, etc. The wood is strong, firm, easily worked and has an attractive grain. The heartwood is usually red whereas the sapwood tends to be yellow to orange.

HEMLOCK
This wood is often called hemlock fir, or even Alaskan hemlock. It is pale yellow to brown, straight-grained and even-textured. Hemlock has all the characteristics of other more common softwoods.

PARANA PINE
The colour ranges from pale yellow to blushes of red. It is even-grained with few knots, carves well and can be bought at most small DIY timber merchants.

YEW
A good, hard, close-grained, lustrous wood, it varies in colour from pale yellow to dark plum red – it is often plain but can be burred and richly figured. It is a good furniture wood and perfect for small carved exhibition pieces.

Hard Woods

APPLE
A good wood for turning – apple is very dense-grained and hard, much used in the past for small domestic kitchenwares.

ASH
The wood of the English ash is long-grained and very tough. It was in the past used for cart and carriage building. In the middle of the nineteenth century imported ash was in common use for bedroom furniture.

CANADIAN BASSWOOD
A very plain wood, very much like lime – works very well, usually a grey/yellow in colour.

BEECH
The wood is close-grained and pale brown-yellow in colour, a good wood to work. It was used in the past for chairs and toys. If cut correctly it is beautifully grained – it is a good wood for small domestic carved ware.

BIRCH
A heavy wood which has yellow sapwood and reddish heartwood. It was used for small turned items such as kitchen treen and bobbins. A pleasant wood to carve and works well.

BOXWOOD
A fine-textured, yellow-brown, heavy wood – when it is carved or turned it gives off a distinctive and very pleasant smell. When it is finely finished it has a natural polished appearance. It can be carved with fine details – it was much used by the Victorians for small domestic and industrial ware such as spinning tops, toys, bowls, shuttles and printers' blocks.

CHERRY
A close-grained, even, brown-red wood. It carves well and was, and still is, used for chairs, brushes, etc.

CHESTNUT
A brown-yellow wood which has many of the characteristics of oak. It was used in the fourteenth and fifteenth centuries for building and roof structures, and in many of our churches and cathedrals the fine carved interior details are of chestnut. It carves well, but there are often problems with ring shakes.

EBONY
A black-brown, sometimes purple, wood, very hard. It carves well but is expensive. If you want the appearance of ebony you can use stained pear wood. At one time ebony was used for furniture, but now supplies are so restricted it is only used for small turned and inlay items such as walking-stick handles, chessmen and fancy boxes.

ENGLISH ELM

A broad-grained, brown-red wood which was much used for coffins and water pumps. It has a most attractive grain but it has a tendency to warp. At this moment there is an abundance of free elm of reasonable quality, the result of the Dutch elm disease outbreak and the necessary felling of a considerable number of our native trees.

HICKORY

Often referred to as red-heart hickory or white sapwood hickory, its widest use is for hammer and pick handles. It is difficult to carve but it has a beautiful surface when cut.

HOLLY

A very white wood which was used for small decorative pieces. English treen makers and European inlay craftsmen used this wood, now only available in small quantities.

IROKO

A Nigerian wood, sometimes known as African teak. A light to dark brown colour, it looks good but is difficult to work.

JARRAH

A very dense Australian 'mahogany'-type wood which takes a fine polish, but is rather coarse-grained. Dark red in colour, it can be obtained in very large pieces.

LIGNUM VITAE

A very heavy tropical American hardwood, mostly used for mallet-heads and small turned work. Black-brown-yellow in colour, it was once a favourite for the small carved and turned items that we now know as treen.

LIME

This wood is a favourite with carvers past and present. It carves well, it is close-grained and hard. It can be easily carved in any direction and was much used by the English carver Grinling Gibbons.

MAHOGANY

Over the last two hundred years this very popular wood has been used for just about everything. There are many varieties such as American or Cuban mahogany, Guatemalan mahogany, African mahogany and many more – they all have slightly different characteristics, but mostly they work well and are pink-brown in colour.

OAK

A very strong wood which was used mainly in churches and cathedrals. Not suitable for fine work as it can be rather coarse, but a good wood for large exhibition pieces.

PEAR

A beautiful wood to carve – it has a short close grain and can be carved in most directions. It was used for many of the small domestic objects such as spoons, cups, bowls, forks, etc.

ROSEWOOD

An exotic, expensive wood which has an ebony-like quality; it is sometimes brown to blackish-purple in colour. Not an easy wood to carve, having a tendency to split along the grain. It was used in the middle of the nineteenth century for pianos and fancy boxes.

SAPELE

Sometimes known as West African or Gold Coast cedar, it has a red-brown colour and a curly grain.

SYCAMORE

A hard, light-coloured wood which has a distinctive grain. As it has no smell or taste it is suitable for kitchenware such as dishes and platters, dairy equipment, rolling pins, etc.

TEAK

Sometimes called Burmese or Indian teak, it is brown in colour and oily in texture. It works well, but will take the edge off all your tools.

WALNUT

In the past this wood was used for church furniture and Georgian interiors. The wood works well and takes a good polish. It has burrs, curls and figures in the grain which make it a good wood for exhibition pieces.

Wood Carving Techniques
Used World-wide

There are as many ways of carving wood as there are carvers, but for the sake of clarity I have organised the main wood carving techniques into four groups.

Most of the pieces that we loosely refer to as 'ethnic carving' are work which has been produced in isolated tribal communities, in America, Africa, Oceania and pre-medieval Europe and Asia. This type of carving, which was created with very basic tools, I refer to as chip, adze and knife work. Many of my references are by necessity generalisations, but my aim is to group carvings by technique and style.

CHIP CARVING
As the name implies, this technique involves the removal of small chips of wood. This is done with simple tools and is usually a method of patterning large areas of flat wood. Nicks or pockets of wood are removed with direct and geometrically repeated cuts. Although chip carving is often described as primitive, this is not at all an

21 Nimba or fertility mask of the Baga tribe, Guinea. This head portion of the feared and respected fertility figure has been sculpted in the round, and then surface chip-carved.

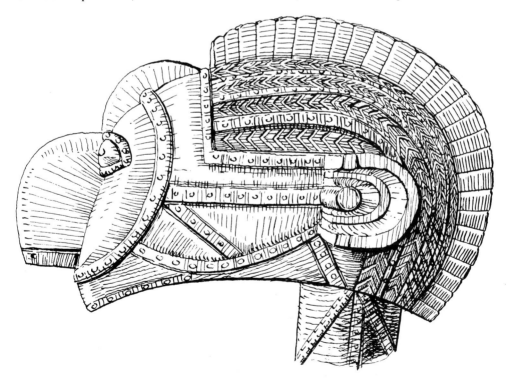

accurate description, as the resultant carvings are often involved, complex and beautifully organised examples of the carver's craft. Chip carving usually refers to a cut pattern which is repeated over large flat areas, but in African and Eastern tribal work three-dimensional figures are sometimes covered with chip-carved decoration. This is a technique which has been used by most wood working communities, and there are some outstanding examples of English, Scandinavian, and North European chip carving, but for the purposes of this book I will be concentrating on the chip carving of Africa, India, the Far East and Oceania.

ADZE AND KNIFE WORK
Adze and knife carvings are those sculptural, symbolistic and representational carvings done by selected tribal societies. Pieces of this type were usually carved with basic adzes, axes and knives, and were rarely made for practical domestic use, being intended more as props, masks and totems for tribal rituals and ceremonies. In these

22　This ethnic Eastern carver is able to support and grip his work with his feet – but then he has probably been carving all his life.

societies, wood, its function and usage, is related to sacred and mythical beliefs. The carver and his method, although they hold an important position in society, are totally dependent on the tribal belief that there are in wood and trees specific spirits and magical powers. The ethnic wood carver uses knife and adze in order to reveal the physical shapes of the spirits that dwell in the wood. The tribal wood carver's aim is not to create a disassociated object like a cupboard or a chair – he is primarily a man of magic.

FLAT CHISEL AND ROUND GOUGE WORK
The marks of the chisel and the gouge can still be seen in some of our churches and cathedrals. Working mainly in oak, the humble carvers did their best to copy the style and form of the more prestigious stone carvers. Gradually however it was realised that wood carving was ideally suited not only for massive structures, but also for interiors and furniture. During the Middle Ages the wood carver did his best to make his work look like stone or metal, but by the end of the fourteenth century the new age of the wood carver had begun. Apart from work commissioned by the churches, very little

23 Ancient Maori carving tools, New Zealand. The large stone would have originally been lashed to the end of a carved wooden handle; the two small stones would most probably be hand held. They are heavy and still have a beautifully keen edge. With primitive tools of this type the Maoris carved sculptures of amazing complexity (*Nottingham Castle Museum*).

has survived from this period, but there is enough to give us a clear picture of the age. Of course most of the carvings were copies of earlier religious themes, so there was little room for self-expression.

As far as the carving techniques are concerned, the carvers used mallet, chisel and gouge to great effect. The fashion for three-dimensional foliage, flowing lines and bold pattern was for the wood carver a good opportunity for craft expression. High up in the roof beams, and hidden away under seats, are many examples of uniquely individual work: the carvers, knowing that these works would rarely be seen, felt that they were able to carve in a way that was unfettered by the religious and craft restrictions of the period. The style of these hidden carvings is unmannered, the workmanship is direct, and the themes are often indications of the earthy lifestyle of the carvers. Over the centuries changing religious and social attitudes have passed these carvings by. They haven't been painted over, removed or changed, so they are for us direct links with craft wood carvers of a past age.

DRILLED AND PIERCED WORK
By about the sixteenth century the European Renaissance was well established and I think it fair to say that the work of the wood carver dominated the art, the architecture and the interiors of the period. Everything was carved, wall panels, door surrounds, stairways, furniture, all worked in a style which can only be described as elaborate and naturalistic. Travel and improved communications gradually brought about a situation where ideas and fashions knew no political or national boundaries. In this new and modern age with its imported woods, its knowledge of a greater world and its flowing styles, carving developed into what has been described as 'an age of the florid, the flamboyant and the vulgar'. In many ways that description does fit the period. Fashions demanded even more realism and excessive pattern but the woodcarvers of the period were equal to the task. They were no longer satisfied to hew naive shapes from massive timbers; they glued, they built up the wood, they drilled and gilded, they used all the

(opposite)
24 Medieval misericord from Lincoln Cathedral. Although these carvings date from the late fourteenth century, the marks of the adze and the chisel can still be clearly seen. A smooth finish must not be confused with a good finish; the first is a sanded, smooth to the touch surface and the second is a visually exciting texture.

25 Carved frame in walnut, by Antonio Barili. Fifteenth century, Siena. Barili carved in a flamboyant style which is reminiscent of the English carver Grinling Gibbons. The winged angel heads and the excess of carved fruit and foliage are a good example of applied and built-up carving.

29

26 Carved walnut armchair. English, 1670.
The flowing style and the 'fleshy' motifs are
almost overwhelming, but the carving techniques of turning and piercing have been adven-
turously explored (*Victoria and Albert Museum,
London*).

tricks of their trade and they reached a standard of workmanship and expertise that has never been bettered. Of the many brilliant carvers of this period, Grinling Gibbons is the most outstanding. He produced so much work that no book on wood carving would be complete without reference to him, his methods and his period.

TURNED AND CARVED FURNITURE AND DOMESTIC WARE

The craft of turning wood on a lathe has been understood and practised for many hundreds of years, but it is only in the last two or three hundred years that it has developed to any great extent. The timber to be turned is pivoted between two points, and while it is spun mechanically, or treadled manually, the turner pushes his cutting chisels and gouges against the wood. Using this wood-working technique we can produce huge corner posts for beds, cupboard legs, chair legs, etc, right down to the minute kitchen and domestic ware that we know collectively as treen. Often the wood to be turned is made from bulky lumps of timber that are built up and glued together. Sometimes this turned wood is left in its smooth turned state, but more often than not it is further carved and worked so that the work of the turner is almost totally concealed. Treen means 'of the trees' and it usually refers to wood ware that is smaller than a chair. A lot of treen was turned and then carved by individual country craftsmen who made very humble utilitarian kitchen and home articles. Some of these

(top)
27 Welsh loving spoon. Nineteenth century. Although this type of treen is known as Welsh work or Loving work, examples of similar carvings can be found in many European countries. The complexities of the knife-carved designs are an expression of the peasant carver's love for his sweetheart.

28 A characteristic example of Tudor turned and carved work. This is a comparatively simple version; many of the more complex are so carved that the original turned post is almost totally obscured (*Quenby Hall, Leicestershire*).

small wooden articles were 'one off', carved in the home by amateurs who were intent on making tokens of love such as spoons or children's toys. The character of these small carvings is by their very nature individual, and free from fashion and style.

Turning developed in the nineteenth century into, on the one hand, a mass-produced furniture style that was amazingly ornate and culminated in that absurdity the Victorian 'whatnot', and on the other hand a whole mass of kitchen, nursery and bedroom paraphernalia of which the gentleman's portable carved wooden egg-cup is a representative example.

INLAY, MARQUETRY, AND TUNBRIDGE WARE

Inlay, marquetry and Tunbridging, are all methods of applying pieces of exotic and decorative wood to the surfaces of more common woods.

Although there are many beautiful examples of ethnic work where inlays of wood, shell, metal and mastic have been used, inlaying and marquetry are considered to be wood carving techniques which relate primarily to the furniture and house interiors of sixteenth, seventeenth and eighteenth century Europe. Elaborate inlay and marquetry became one of the most characteristic

29 This nineteenth century butter mould, carved in lime, is quite deeply worked – the thistle motif was in common use throughout the Victorian period. Most of the carvings that were used in the preparation of food were carved from lime, because it was odourless and tasteless (*Rutland County Museum*).

(*opposite*)
30 (A) Drawing out the design. (B) Cutting out the design with a fine craft knife. (C) The stencil is carefully taped in place and then painted with a thin, coloured, water wash. (D) The edges of the design are marked in with vertical, controlled, chisel cuts. (E) The coloured portion of the design is flat-carved to a depth of about 3–4 cm. (F) The bold surface of the wood is worked with a punch.

With all wood carving the work in the initial design stage is the most critical – it is vital that the positive and negative areas of the design are equally balanced.

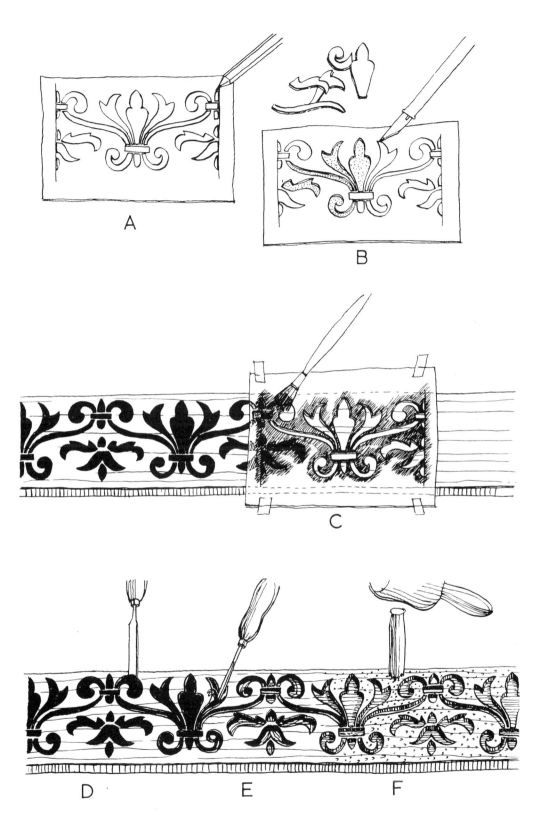

A

B

C

D   E   F

features of the Romantic Renaissance furniture design style. The subtleties of pattern, the unfamiliar wood figures, and the complexities of the method, are factors which were only made possible by global trade, and rapid technological achievement.

For wood craft culmination these methods of wood decoration are valid and important elements which should be experienced for balanced development.

How to Prepare the Wood and Lay Out the Patterns

It is essential that the wood to be carved is free from foreign bodies such as nails, paint and dirt – the wood must be clean and firmly positioned. It is important that your carving is planned; it is no good just cutting away the wood and hoping for the best. Drawing is so important that it is worth a special mention. Always have a sketch book at hand and sketch as much as possible. When you have decided what it is you want to carve, then you must decide on scale and whether it is going to be a low-relief or three-dimensional and sculptural. Lastly you must choose a wood that is going to fit your style and pocket – it is always good policy to buy the best wood that you can afford. When you are choosing a piece, don't be rushed, take your time and consider its faults and qualities. It sometimes helps if you make a miniature of the proposed carving out of a piece of plastic clay or soap. This will give you some idea of what the finished carving will look like when it is 'in the round'.

If your subject is going to be sculptural, you will have to draw out the figure on all sides of the wood. This drawing can be done by eye or, if the subject is small, then you can do the preliminary designs on tracing paper and transfer them through to the wood.

If your proposed carving is a panel or a repeated moulding, it would be best if you first of all worked out the designs on tracing paper. Once you have decided which part of the design is to be cut away, these areas must be shaded in on the preliminary design, sketched and then carefully cut out. The paper pattern is then stuck or taped to the wood, and with a stencil brush the design can be marked in with a thick water paint – obviously you must only colour in the areas that are to be cut away.

With large sculptural works there is no particular benefit in laboriously removing large areas of unwanted wood with a mallet and chisel. It is much more to the point if they are cut away with a band saw or small coping saw. If you are going to cut away large areas of wood it is even more important that you are sure in your own mind that you have fully considered the finished carving. At all stages in your work it is vital that you stand back and view the carving from as many angles as possible.

With very large works it is often better if the wood to be carved is placed on the floor and cut with an adze. For adze work I would advise you to wear boots or shin pads, but at the very least, brace the work with your foot, and be sure to give it your full attention. At the risk of repeating myself, it is vital that you do as many sketches as time allows and always refer to as many museum pieces as possible. This doesn't mean that you should copy old work, but it does mean that you should use them for technique and method reference.

A knowledge of technical drawing is very useful – but enough for me to finish by saying that good drawing is the essence of good and considered carving.

2

CHIP CARVING, ADZE AND KNIFE WORK

Two of the oldest wood carving tools known to man are the adze and the knife. Over the years these have been developed so that there are now hundreds of different types, but basically the design and the uses to which they are put remain the same.

Adze Work

The adze looks like a marriage between a hoe and an axe. In use it is swung and the wood is removed in scooped shell-shaped curls. The metal head of the adze is heavy, concave, razor-sharp and fixed to a long wooden shaft. The carver holds the handle or shaft with two hands, and when he swings it like a pendulum, the weight of the metal head and the cutting action of the concave blade result in a recognisable, characteristic adzed finish. On old English, European and modern ethnic carvings, the marks left by the adze can clearly be seen and because there is little attempt to go over the surface

with a finer cutting tool, the honesty and simplicity of the original design cannot be questioned. Many medieval wood carvings were originally painted with brilliant primary colours, and when the Puritans and then the Victorians decided to 'clean them up', a great number of adze carvings were lost.

This efficient cutting tool was especially useful when a lot of wood had to be removed quickly, with little effort. We now live in a society where superficial finish and effect are the order of the day, so if we wanted to see the adze at work it would be necessary to visit the ethnic carvers of Africa or America.

ETHNIC ADZE WORK
The cutting of large areas of wood is best done with the adze – a skilled carver works rhythmically and apparently mechanically. The swing of the carver's arm brings the adze in smooth controlled arcs and guides the tool up and down, or backwards and for-

31   Detail from door post (*right*) and lintel from a Maori meeting house, New Zealand. The carving methods used are piercing and surface chip work.

wards, across the surface of the wood. The physical position the carver takes is one of the factors responsible for the characteristic patterns that appear on the surface of adzed wood.

When you first carve with an adze, it will feel strange and it is likely that your work will need sanding or tidying up with a rasp or some such tool. Your aim should be to work the surface so that the tool leaves rhythmic scallops; these, when you have developed sufficient skill, will add to the wholeness of your technique.

There are adze-type tools which have a head with two holes. The head can be turned round so that the blade is either vertical or horizontal – so it can be used as an axe or an adze. Adze work as seen on ethnic carving is very crisp, smooth and ordered, this of course relates to the skill of the carver, but I would say that it has more to do with the carver's appreciation of the limitations of the wood and the tool. As a broad generalisation the adze is best used for work that is large, sculptural and generously curved.

NORTH AMERICAN INDIAN CARVING
The Indians of the north-west coast of America, living on a strip of land which runs from the Columbia river in the south to Alaska in the north, were fortunate in having on one side a sea which provided them with an almost unlimited supply of salmon and herring. During the season they could easily catch and preserve enough food for the rest of the year, leaving them plenty of time for other activities. They were also in the happy situation of being surrounded by vast cedar forests, which gave them wood

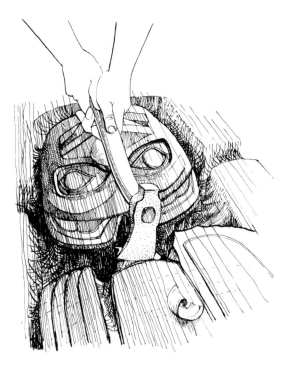

(*top*)
32   The carved wooden chests and boxes made by the Indians of the American North West Coast were sewn together with gut and leather thongs. Holes were first made with the primitive twist drill – notice how the box panel is fixed to the log by means of a peg and cord clamp.

33   A two-handed modern adze with a metal head. Most of the Indian totem carving is in deep relief, a mixture of adze and chisel carving. The motifs are lined and painted in with primary colours.

(*left*)
34 North West Coast – Haida house post. A house and clan totem which illustrates the myth of an Indian woman being carried away by a killer whale. There is some confusion as to the real interpretation of these motifs; even Indian experts from the same tribe come up with differing explanations.

35 The clan and myth orientated Haida Indians of the North West Coast lived in thriving communities up until the beginning of the nineteenth century, but increased communications with traders led to a decline in their social traditions and crafts. The designs on their totems began to weaken and the introduction of better tools led to the breaking down of their time-proven carving methods.

for their homes, their weapons and their furniture.

In the long dark winter the whole tribe became absorbed in playing out a supernatural and dramatic ritual. For this sacred period names were changed, special clothes were worn, and prestigious gifts exchanged. Clan and social prestige were obtained by possessing and giving objects which were not only beautiful but endowed with mythological powers. Clan crests and masks were adopted and families marked their social rise, their ancestry and their entitlement by carrying new totems.

The majority of these objects were made from the easily carved and worked cedar wood. These carvings not only took the form of giant totem poles, but also domestic items such as bowls, boxes and furniture. There is some evidence of early primitive stone and bone carving, but the wood carving probably only really started with the introduction of European iron and steel knives and axes.

The carved designs are all heraldic and totemic in nature, but in most examples the patterns and designs have been so abstracted that the original animal or mythological

36 A beautiful three-dimensional North West Coast Indian grease bowl. The design is characteristic of middle nineteenth century work. The bird motif is the most common, but other forms are seals, ducks, wolves and fish – in almost all cases the head of the animal is carved so that it becomes the handle of the bowl (*Horniman Museum, London*).

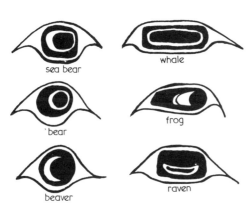

37 A yellow cedar or yew steamed and bent box. The curved corners and the concave sides are formed partly by the carving and partly by the fact that the box was formed out of a single piece of wood. The raven design is typical, with the beak on one end, the tail on the other and stylised wings and feet on the side panels.

(*left*)
38 Stylised eye motifs.

sea bear

whale

bear

frog

beaver

raven

39 The carving on all the North West Coast boxes is in shallow relief, hardly more than slight chip-carved lines. It is the painting and design arrangement that gives an illusion of depth.

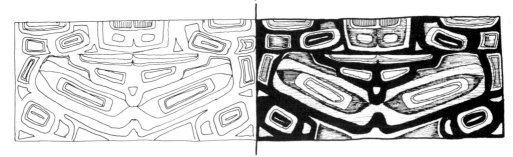

40 A most perfect Tsimshian or Haida mask. Originally this would have been vividly painted with tribal clan designs. The knot-free, straight-grained cedar is the best wood for this type of work (*Horniman Museum, London*).

beast forms can hardly be recognised. The totem poles give the illusion that they are deeply carved and undercut, but in many instances they are deeply incised rather than carved. The tools used are simple and basic, the adze, the axe and the knife, but with these the straight-grained and knot-free cedar wood is easily worked. The design motifs are nearly always copied from masters or templates; although the basic designs are adapted to suit the shape of the object being carved, the total concept of the original design is always preserved.

The Kwakiutl, Haida and Tlingit Indians of this coast were indeed fortunate in being free for a great part of the year to indulge in activities unrelated to obtaining food. Also they had an unlimited supply of wood which was perfect for carving. These two factors were not in themselves enough to produce the fantastic carvings; their main motivation was the indulgent, extravagant and ritualised potlatch or giving ceremonies.

In this society the carvers of wood became as important as, say, the masons and carvers of fourteenth-century Europe. In the same way the carvers simplified the carvings until the designs were reduced to abstracted shapes. These Indian wood carvings became so conventionalised that they divided the animals into simple design elements, such as 'nostril', 'eye', 'paws', etc, freeing shapes and designs from unnecessary minutiae. As the carvings were often used as props in the ritualised dramas, it was important that they conveyed the message directly.

The carved totems and masks, especially those intended for use at ceremonies, were painted, inlaid and sometimes made of several hinged parts. These 'working' carvings were worn at the dances and mimes. At the pull of a string, wooden wings would flap, or the beak would move. Of late there has been a revival of interest in these carvings, and descendants of the old carvers are again being commissioned to carve new totems and ritual regalia.

ADZE CARVING YOUR OWN TOTEM
For this project you will need either a large section from a soft pine tree, or a piece of an

41   A cradle or support of this type can easily be knocked up out of scrap timber. The wood you are working must be accessible, but secure.

42   If you prefer, the wood can be supported on a horizontal floor cradle. This is much easier to make, but it takes up more room and is not quite as flexible.

A   B   C

43   (A) The totem is first of all sketched and considered, then the basic design areas are drawn in with chalk. (B) Many of the preliminary cuts can be made with a saw. (C) The whole essence of totem carving is that the majority of the work is in relief; the feeling of depth is achieved by careful design work and surface outlining.

old telegraph pole. It does sound rather ambitious but I assure you that if you call on your local telephone installations office, or search your local demolition yard, you will come up with just the thing. In section the wood needs to be about 32 cm across and about 2 metres in height. You will find that a piece of wood of this size can be lifted and transported if you have a strong willing friend.

The piece of wood that I have suggested has roughly the same proportions as the average human figure, so it seems logical that we should attempt to carve such a figure. As the pole is heavy it isn't going to do much moving about. It needs to be placed in a position that is safe, stable and sheltered. The garage would seem to be the place, but if you have a shed, so much the better. There are several points to consider when you are stabilizing your piece of wood: do you want it on the floor so that you can attack it from above, or do you want it leaning against a wall so that it is more or less standing upright?

If you have a two-handed adze rather like a small tree axe it would make things a lot easier if the subject to be carved is below your waist height; this would allow the momentum and weight of the adze to do most of the work. If you have a small single-handed adze I would suggest that you lean the piece of wood against the wall, and fix it so that it cannot roll from side to side, or slide towards you. As you can see from my drawings there are several ways of making a cradle to hold the work.

Once the wood is secure you can begin – with a carving of these proportions, you will need to be direct, but organised. The figure that I decided to carve was in many ways similar to an American totem, in as much as the main features such as the eyes, mouth and nose are exaggerated. You must also decide whether or not it is going to be naked or in costume; if you decide on the latter then you will also have to consider the costume, perhaps relating it to the traditional North American Indian costume of the period – the choice is yours.

When you have researched the figure and the costume and are ready to begin, you will need to rough out the design on the wood. In the early stages it is probably best if the design is drawn in with chalk, pencil or water paint. Don't put anything on the wood that is going to leave a permanent stain. Mark in all the areas that have to be cut away, and also mark in any cuts that can be made directly with a saw. You will see from the drawing that with a figure of this character, although the final sculpture will be three-dimensional, and will be able to be seen from all angles, the actual carving is only in shallow relief – it is the manner of the under-cuts that give an illusion of depth.

Once you have made your preliminary saw cuts, you have to cut down, and in, with the cut between you and the adze. You will get to a point where you will have to approach the work from the other end, but by that time the piece of wood will have lost a fair amount of weight, and it should be more manageable.

Traditionally carvings of this kind were brought to a very fine finish and then painted, so you must, quite early on, decide

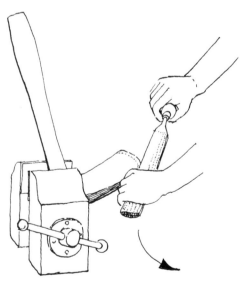

44 An adze is a difficult tool to sharpen; the concave blade can either be removed from the handle and then ground on revolving stone, or better still gripped in the vice as indicated, and brought to an angle of 5°–10° with a large, curved section, mill file.

how your carving is to be treated. If the carving is going to be positioned indoors, perhaps in an entrance hall, it will usually need to be fairly smooth. It can be finished with a chisel, sanded and finally sealed. If on the other hand you want it to stand at the far end of the garden, then it will need a treatment that protects it from the weather.

If you choose to paint it in a traditional totem fashion, then the colours will need to be primary rather than secondary. Bring the wood to a fine finish with sandpaper or a scraper, and then give it a seal. You can now begin the painting – if you study the original carvings you will see that it is the proud surfaces that are painted and then lined in with a hard dark line. When you have finished the painting and it is dry, you can apply another coat of sealer.

TIPS ON USING AN ADZE

One or two tips about using an adze. If you have the correct tool, and they can be easily obtained if you go to a good merchant, the head of the adze will be heavy and very sharp, so it has to be used with considerable care. In usage an adze has to be swung down and towards you; obviously this can be tricky, but as long as you are working within your own capabilities there should be no problems.

The sharpening of an adze will need a different approach than say sharpening a chisel, but the theory is basically the same. The adze is gripped firmly in a vice with the inside of the curved blade uppermost. Then, using a large mill file, the cutting edge can be brought to an angle of 5 to 10°. Finally with fine whetting you can bring the blade up to a good edge.

Chip Carving

This is one of the most beautiful techniques used by the wood carver. It is a relatively simple process, in which the surface of the wood is organised into a grid, and with a simple tool, such as a knife, the carver removes small nicks of wood. This technique is especially favoured by ethnic wood carvers, and for them it is usually a method

45 Characteristic Oceanic chip-carved designs – all of which can be achieved with the simplest of chisels or knives.

46 These early chip-carved motifs are known as 'roses' and they are commonly found on European thirteenth century chests. The technique is based on simple triangular cuts, but the resulting carvings look very complex.

of patterning large areas of flat wood. Once the surface to be cut is drawn out in a grid, the nicks or pockets of wood are removed with a series of direct and repeated cuts. This characteristic method of carving is created by the shape of the cutting edge – for example the gouge cuts little moon shapes, the corner of a chisel cuts little triangles, and so on.

In the text books this technique usually comes under the heading of primitive carving, the name obviously describing its source rather than its effectiveness. Many examples of chip carving are very simple, others are complex and involved, but the resultant works can be really beautiful, highly organised examples of the carver's craft.

On English medieval and European wood carving one of the most effective of the chip carving motifs is the stylised rose; it commonly appears on chests, tables, bench ends, etc. On Oceanic carvings it is nearly always an overall patterning technique, which in its most usual form is repeated columns of shallow triangular cuts.

Carving of this character can be found in most wood carving societies, England, Scandinavia, Northern Europe, etc, but by far the most exciting occur on many of the primitive sculptural works of Africa and Oceania.

AFRICAN CHIP CARVING

In many African tribal societies trees are believed to be the homes of gods and spirits – this is one of the reasons that most of the religious and ritual articles are made of wood. Of course as wood is so easily obtained it is also used for the more mundane objects such as weapons, doors, bowls and small items of furniture. It has been suggested that of all the African arts and crafts wood carving is the most highly developed, and the most valued. In European and Western societies the carver of wood is considered to be a humble workman, but in African tribal societies he is a person of importance and rank.

Traditionally the carving was achieved using small single-hand adzes and curved double-edged knives. The objects were first

45

47   A bed from Mo Telemark, Norway. The
design motifs are variations on the Gothic 'rose'
or 'sun'; the twined knots are common on North
European carved work and were a special favourite on very early Norse work. Once again the technique used is simple chip carving; the skill lies in
the initial design conception.

48   Yoruba carver, Nigeria, polishing the wood
with the side of the knife. While he works he grips
the carving between his knees, or rests it on his
lap – he applies pressure on the flat of the knife
blade with his left thumb. Work of this size and
type is first of all roughed out with the adze.

of all roughed out with the adze and then finished and patterned with the knife. Many of the figures are so stylised and abstracted that they can only really be understood and appreciated by the carver and the society in which he works.

A characteristic of the tribal carvings are the chip-carved patterns that swirl over and decorate most of the surface of the wood. Obviously the patterns and designs are a direct result of the performance of the simple knives and chisels, but having said that, it is of interest to know why there is such a mass of pattern. In cultures that place such emphasis on body decoration, scarification and complex hair arrangements, it is not surprising that the wood-carved designs on the sculptures are pattern-related. It is thought that the designs are straightforward pattern impressions inspired by dress and tribal markings. The chip carving doesn't necessarily have to be in the form of separate 'nicks', it can be organised so that the wood is lined and furrowed.

Some of the tribes are recognised as being particularly 'carved-wood conscious', and of these the Dogons and the Baga are for us in a class of their own. The wood carvings have

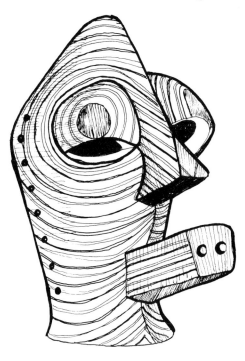

49 Royal statue, Dengese, Congo, African. This sculpture is nearly as high as a man. The chip-carved designs are inspired by Dengese body scarification.

(*right*)
50 Basongye, Congo. Masks of this character inspired the Cubists at the beginning of the twentieth century. Both Braque and Picasso were profoundly moved by what came to be known as 'African Primitives'.

51   Funerary Screen, Ijo. As European wood
working techniques and tools were introduced
into Africa, so the quality of the carving deterio-
rated. This screen clearly shows a break away
from the earlier carving traditions. The heads,
limbs, torsos, are all made as separate pieces and
linked up at a later stage.

48

52 Wooden mask, Zaire – Songye. Without the chip-carved lines this mask would be almost shapeless. Objects of this type were used as 'stage props' by the witch doctor and it is interesting to see how a relatively simple carving can be transformed into a work of power and vitality by the use of surface pattern (*Horniman Museum, London*).

53 This chip-carved paddle, probably from
Africa, illustrates how ancient designs can be
influenced by modern ideas – in this case the old
'crocodile' and 'flower' motives have been linked
up with a typical Victorian clock face. The chip-
carved lines are emphasised by being filled in
with a white mastic (*Nottingham Castle
Museum*).

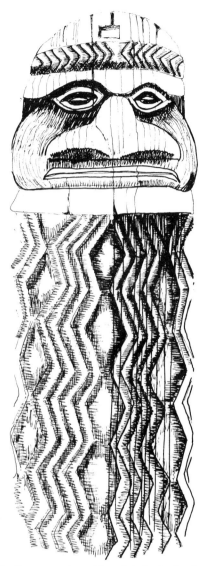

54 A chip-carved paddle handle from the Astral Islands, Oceania. The figures on the handles are called Tiki, which means creator. Although the pattern looks unbelievably complex, it is created by the removal of horizontally organised triangular chips. Although like a paddle in shape, objects of this character were used to place gifts on the sacred altars.

55 Door post from New Caledonia. In character this carving is very much like the totems of North America – the pattern owes much to smaller chip-carved designs. The height is about 3 metres so it was probably carved with a knife and adze.

many functions, usages and meanings – they are sometimes signs of rank, symbols of prestige and other times objects that have religious and fetish significance – but be they bowls, masks or figures they are always prized possessions.

OCEANIC WOOD CARVING

'Oceanic' usually refers to the mass of islands in the Pacific which are east of Malaysia. The wood carvings of these islands are amazingly 'organised' and complex – this is cause for wonder when it is realised that most of them were done with such simple tools as the shell and stone bladed adze and the bone knife. The culture and economy of those islanders is based on hunting, fishing and small homestead gardens. Most of the objects of everyday life have to be self-made and decorated, so working in wood is not necessarily a specialist task. This generally means that day-to-day articles such as bowls, dishes, boxes, etc, are made in the home, while masks, boats and objects of religious significance are made and carved by professionals.

56 Chip-carved club from Fiji. The photograph illustrates the 'business' end of the club. With this particular design the 'negative' background grid is cut away. In other carvings from the same area, the little 'positive' octagons are cut away leaving a surface line and square pattern (*Nottingham Castle Museum*).

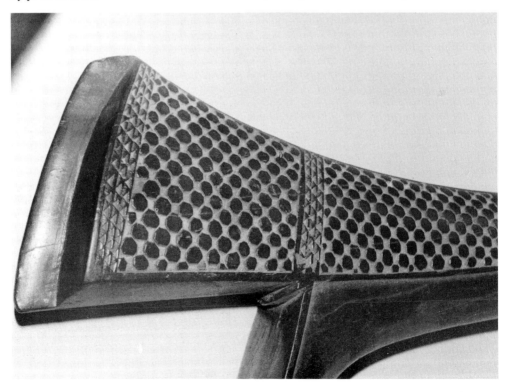

57 A club from Samoa. The chip-carved design exploits the triangle motif; the cut-away pattern is filled with a white mastic. Most of these Oceanic carvings are on heavy, dense, hard wood which is straight-grained and knot-free.

The carvings are designed to set motifs and conform to accepted codes of practice, so there is little room for artistic self-expression. Usually the carving relates either to weapons or magic, so the patterns are always significant. Gradually metal tools are replacing the traditional ones and this is slowly changing the wood carving techniques. The most common carving method was shallow relief work, but with the introduction of more efficient tools the patterns are becoming deeper and more three-dimensional.

One of the most interesting and elaborate forms of wood carving expression is found on the prows of the canoes, on door-surrounds and boat equipment. The designs are usually chip-carved and geo-metric – that is to say the designs are made up of circles, curves and crossed lines. The technique is relatively simple – using either a knife or a chisel, small cuts are made and pieces of wood removed. In this particular instance, the carving technique is secondary to the design concept, and is ideally suited for patterning the large surfaces of the

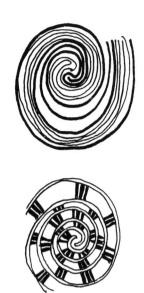
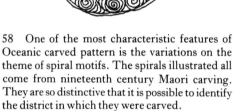

58 One of the most characteristic features of Oceanic carved pattern is the variations on the theme of spiral motifs. The spirals illustrated all come from nineteenth century Maori carving. They are so distinctive that it is possible to identify the district in which they were carved.

59 This chip-carved and pierced door lintel from an early nineteenth century Maori house indicates the importance of the spiral to the Maori craftsmen. Almost all the figures are related to spiral forms.

60 The head of a club, Tonga. The carvers from the Samoa-Tonga area chip-carved their weapons with patterns organised into fields of parallel zigzag lines. Another distinctive feature of Tonga carving is the fact that the chip-carved ground area of the design is linked together so that the uncarved portion of the wood becomes positive pattern (*Nottingham Castle Museum*).

wood. As a generalisation Oceanic wood carvings are, in their total and finished state, works of baffling complexity; but looked at minutely, they can usually be broken down into areas of very simple and basic chip carving.

CHIP CARVING – A GUIDE
For this project I suggest that you use a piece of wood that has been made up into something else, and then decorate the surface. For example you could decorate a small cupboard, the edge of a shelf, the borders of a solid-panelled door, etc. First of all select your object, and then make sure that it is indeed solid wood; it is no good trying to carve a piece of veneered blockboard. It is often possible to obtain cheaply at an auction a good solid piece of furniture, say a chair or a cupboard, and this would be ideal. I will be describing the carving of a front door.

Once you have chosen the object to be carved, work out some method of keeping it steady – with my door it is a simple matter to fix it to the bench with a couple of G clamps. Something like a chair or a cupboard might present problems, and indeed if the article is large and heavy enough, its own weight might keep it in position.

Choose simple designs, such as repeated lines of border pattern; do not be too ambitious. It is most important that you mark and measure out the wood correctly, especially if you are going to do a pattern that relies on single sharp-edge repeated cuts that are all of the same scale and which are going to meet in the thickness of the wood. The chip of wood should always come out cleanly, there should be no need to sand, poke or scrape the surface of the wood at a later stage. If you find that the 'nicks' of wood do not come away cleanly, it probably means that you have drawn out the design too large, or that your cutting tools need a new edge.

You will see from the illustrations that the scope of pattern depends on the chisel, gouge or knife that you are using – but in all cases the method is the same. Press the cutting edge straight down into the wood. For this the tool should be held as near vertical as possible. Then the tool is held flat.

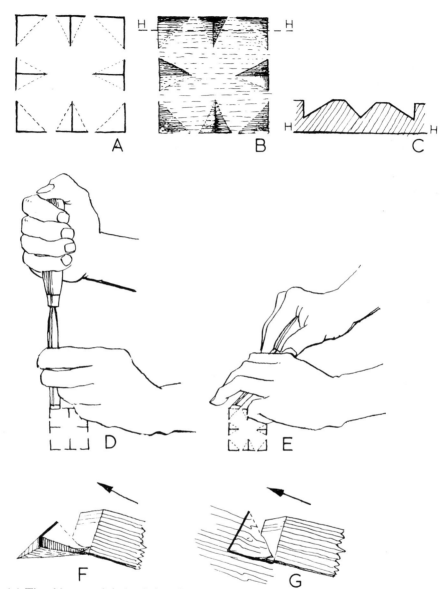

61 (A) The chip-carved design is based on an overall square motif, which is itself composed of regular triangular cuts. The dark lines indicate cuts which have been made with the full width of the chisel, which go vertically into the wood. (B) The finished motif. (C) Section through motif. (D) All the chip-carved triangles are composed of two vertical chisel cuts. (E) If the chisel is sharp, the triangular chips which make up the corners of the square motifs can be removed with three cuts. (F) Only half the width of the blade is used, and the triangular chip is cut away in two halves. (G) The chips must be cut away in the direction of the grain.

(left)
62 Chip-carved design on a panelled door. This illustration shows how important it is that the chip-carved motifs are organised on a well drawn grid. Before any cuts are made I suggest that you practise the technique on a piece of scrap wood.

(right)
63 Detail from an Oceanic ceremonial adze handle. The carver of wood in most pre-twentieth century Oceanic societies was a man of importance, and it is most probable that the adze was a symbolistic badge of office. This particular adze which is almost 150 cm in length would have been carried on prestigious occasions. The handle, which is square in section, is pierced and deeply carved, and finally the surface is cut with deep chip-carved designs (*Nottingham Castle Museum*).

with the surface secondary cuts made so that the cutting edge meets the primary cut. The chip of wood should now fall free.

Tips: Do not work beyond your skill – choose a knot-free wood – and do not try to cut too deeply.

57

3

FLAT CHISEL AND ROUND
GOUGE WORK

At the end of the fourteenth and at the beginning of the fifteenth century England and Europe were going through a period of revolution and social change. A wealthy middle class was emerging and for various reasons related to protection and power they were forming themselves into highly organised trade guilds. These factors combined to bring in an age of stability and progress. It was as if England and Europe were climbing out of a dark period which had begun a thousand years before, when the Romans left. Improved trade, faster communications and a wealthy ruling merchant class created an age of artistic enlightenment. These 'new rich' wanted bigger houses, better trade halls, more comfortable churches and grander cathedrals. Wood was plentiful, tools were improved, so for the workers in wood it was a period of expansion and renewed creativity. Everywhere large churches were being built, not in the small and cramped style of the past, but with seats, screens, pulpits and wood-lined interiors.

All these conditions gave the wood carver the opportunity to display his skills. The establishment of the time demanded comfort and modern, flowing style, but they also wanted the design themes in the churches to relate to religious and sacred subjects. The carvers were therefore more or less limited to the themes imposed upon them, or suggested by religious dogma. There were exceptions to these conditions, which give us a rare and revealing picture of the mentality and methods of the wood carvers, and of the everyday events of the period.

MISERICORDS – TO HAVE MERCY . . .
The monks and priests had to attend very long services so they devised a shelf on the underside of the hinged bench seats. This meant that while appearing to be standing up, the priests were able to rest their rear ends. As these little shelves or misericords were hidden from general view, and meant for such a lowly purpose it was felt that design themes of high church thinking were unsuitable. The carvers were able to carve

64   Hand-holds from medieval church pews, Cornwall.

58

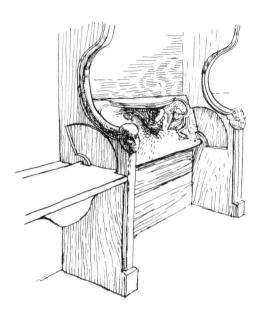

(top)
65   The carved misericords can be seen when the choir stall seats are raised. They form part of a small projecting bracketed shelf on which the less robust monks were able to rest. The essence of misericords is that although the monks were able to take the weight off their feet, they still looked as if they were standing.

(centre)
66   This particular misericord, which is now in the Victoria and Albert Museum, London, illustrates very nicely a wood carver's workshop of the medieval period.

(bottom)
67   This misericord depicts the romance of Alexander; he is seated in a basket and being carried by two hungry griffins. In the legend the griffins carry him so that he can look over the edge of the flat earth. (The carved spear on which Alexander held food up for the griffins has unfortunately broken off.)

68 Misericord, early sixteenth century. St Mary Magdalene, Newark. This misericord illustrates two bears, and a tree which is badly damaged. The marks left by the carver's tools can be clearly seen – there has been no attempt at polishing or refinement. Many of these carvings were, up until the early eighteenth century, left in the raw white wood state.

almost anything that struck their fancy. With this unique opportunity for self-expression the carvers carved just about everything – simple scenes of domestic life, sports, rude tales and popular romances.

Sometimes these carvings are technically crude, but generally they are of a very high standard. Using oak and sometimes elm, and with refined mallets, chisels, gouges and drills, the carvers took the craft to its very limits. The whole area of misericord and bench-end carvings has in the past been described by art and craft critics as grotesque and obscene, but they are honest reflections of the life of the times. From the carpenter's point of view the misericord is a narrow shelf which needs a support or bracket on its underside. In the early instances these brackets were simple plain angles of wood, but the tradition developed of always organising them along certain lines. When we refer to a misericord, it is the carved bracket underneath the shelf that is the focus of our attention. The carving has to

69   This rather lewd misericord illustrates the
'hen-pecked husband' who is being 'debagged'
and thrashed by his wife. In scenes of this type
the bullied husband is nearly always shown
winding wool on a niddy noddy – it is as if the act
of winding wool is a symbol of submissive
domestication. There are all sorts of 'bits and
pieces' missing from many early misericords, so
it must be assumed that prudes from later centuries trimmed them up.

70   This misericord depicts the capture of a
unicorn – the supporters are in the form of mythical beasts. It was said that the unicorn, who sym-
bolised Christ, could only be caught or
approached by a virgin. In this particular scene
the unicorn has placed its head in the virgin's lap,
and so fallen prey to the hunter.

71 Misericord, early sixteenth century. St Mary Magdalene, Newark. This particular carving is a really fine example of Jack-in-the-Green, or Green Man. The face with a sprig of green in its mouth relates to pre-Christian nature worship, and it is thought it may have originated with the earlier Roman Floralia.

be small, and by reasons of design and structure is nearly always triangular, with one side of the triangle forming the underside of the shelf or corbel. The moulded edges of the corbel usually curve down and round the carved bracket, so as to form scrolled bunches of foliage – these are usually referred to as 'supporters'.

The design themes of the carvers are nearly always expressions of good against evil. The carved picture might be a direct lift from a bible story, showing for instance Adam and Eve, or the carver's impression of a dramatic tale like St George and the Dragon. The carvings are usually in deep relief and carved from the same lump of wood as the seat – this meant that the carver would be working with a slab of oak which was at least four or five inches thick. I would say that the main characteristic of this period, so far as wood carving technique is concerned, is the fact that the carvings are taken from massive timber balks; there is no timber fabrication.

CHURCH BENCH OR PEW-ENDS

Seats in churches developed from the uncomfortable stone column slab surrounds and backless bench-stools; once they were wooden, slightly raised off the damp floors, and had high sides and backs to keep out the draught, they offered obvious scope for decoration. The main function of a bench-end is to support the weight of the thick plank seats and backs, and they are often made from single balks of oak anything up to six inches in thickness. The carved motifs on these massive timbers are in many ways similar to those on carved stone, and sometimes the designs are direct copies.

Gradually however a style was developed which was totally individual and more related to the purpose. Unlike the misericords, the vertical bench-ends were in full view of the congregation, so it was felt that they should be carved with strong religious and moral themes. The patterns of the period tended to be simple naturalistic impressions of foliage, but the variations on the foliage theme were enormous. Towards the end of the fourteenth century the foliage designs became more exaggerated until the leaves were almost totally imaginative and unrelated to nature.

Through the fifteenth century the quality of the carving became more and more flowing and generous in character, until the church architecture was almost dominated by wood carving. The art of the wood carver as expressed in the carving of the bench-ends became varied, fanciful and a wonderful medium for free expression. The

(*top*)
72 This design sketch has been taken from a Cornish (England) church bench or pew-end. It has been carved out of a solid slab of oak which must have been at least 10 cm thick. The flowing lines of the motif indicate a strong Renaissance influence.

(*right*)
73 Large figures of this character are common only on the early West Country bench-ends – their size and detail are really exciting and for the student wood carver the style and spirit of the work must surely be inspirational. The cut of the costume, and the design of the instrument indicate that it is Tudor.

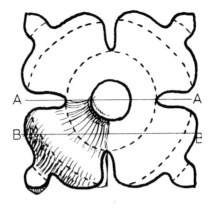

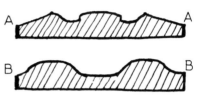

74 This photograph, of the back and front of a sixteenth century Dutch pew-end, shows clearly the carving method. The carvers of the period worked with an economy of style that must be admired and perhaps emulated (*Victoria and Albert Museum, London*).

amount of pattern and the carved story, fable and bible tales reached a peak of beauty that has never since been equalled. The bench-ends were often, it must be supposed, carved by humble village and small-town craftsmen who saw the world through innocent and child-like eyes. The variation of pattern, subject matter and technique is almost endless, and it is this that for the student of wood carving is so exciting.

Using chisels and gouges, the bench-ends and hand-holds were deeply carved and undercut. There are animals, figures and scenes which are 'direct', and carved straight out of the wood without thought to an over-developed and preconceived style. For the carver, the bench-ends can be seen as models of technique and inspiration. The carving methods are straightforward enough; it is the choice of shape and design that is so perfect. The forms on the top rails of the bench-ends are designed to be held and grasped in the hands of people who are pulling themselves up and out of their seats after a long and perhaps cold service. They could have been straight functional forms but the carvers saw fit to make them the object of visual and mental contemplation, as well as shapes that are just asking to be touched. As the carving was going to get a great deal of rubbing and wear it was import-ant that the designs were rounded rather than projecting and sharp. The subjects chosen are so often humorous that it leads me to think that the carver was just enjoying himself and having a bit of fun.

Church furniture was functional, in that it offered protection from damp, leaky roofs, draughts and the cold – but it was also educational, the carvings being one of the means that the clergy used to remind an illi-terate congregation of stories in the Bible and give them examples of correct religious behaviour. .

75 The stylised 'rose' – a common motif which is found on church furniture of many periods. Two circles are cut with the gouge, and then the petal joints are cut. This very simple and direct carving technique results in 'petals' that appear to undulate.

76 Many of the small motifs are straightfor-ward expressions of the shapes, curves and angles of the various cutting tools.

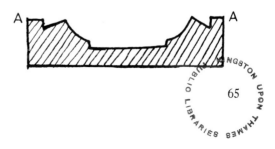

77 Many of the carved hand-holds on medieval bench-ends are designed as warnings to the sinful – some of them are so frightful that I would think twice before I touched them. This particular example shows a spotted ape-like devil stuffing a mitred clergyman into the mouth of hell. Carved hand-holds are of special interest as they are three-dimensional and therefore say more about early carving techniques.

The style of the medieval carving varies from county to county – so much so that we are now able to identify a piece of pew or bench-end carving by its design. In the Western counties of England the bench-ends tend to be plain and square-topped, whereas the Eastern counties have carving full of humour with imaginative and individual carved pictures, and decorated 'poppy-head' tops. There are fables, dogs, devils, virgins, lions, mermaids, monkeys, camels, kings, angels, the list is endless and of course all these figures and animals relate to the period when they were carved. The knights, jesters, etc, are in the costume of the age, and the scenes of everyday life are an insight into customs and occupations of the period.

At the end of the fifteenth century however the style of carving became so elaborate that pattern was used for pattern's sake, so that the designs became dissociated and were no longer personal expressions of the craftsmen. This in turn led to a period when carving became so devoid of growth and new ideas that it was almost totally given over to repetition and unrelated motifs.

Chisel and Gouge Carving in the Round

There are three main carving techniques used in medieval church work: low relief, when the subjects to be carved can only be viewed from one angle and are mostly joined or attached to a panel background, deep or high relief, when the carving is undercut and almost detached from its background, and three-dimensional in-the-round carving, which is free-standing and can be viewed from all sides.

In this project we are going to concentrate on a three-dimensional carving that has its inspirational roots in the bench-end hand-holds of the medieval period. Technically we will use a method of carving which although it is organised, leaves some room for direct carving and development.

First of all you must choose your subject. It needn't relate to church carving, but it would be an advantage if it had the same freedom of style. As you can see from the

78 This early sixteenth century carved hand-hold from St Mary Magdalene, Newark, is a beautifully finished devil or spotted ape. Years of hot hands, and oil lamps have given it a patina which cannot be imitated.

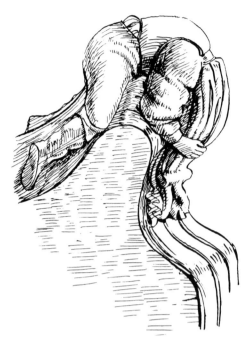

79 This bench-end hand-hold from Winchester Cathedral has in my opinion captured the mood of the medieval period. It is amusing but at the same time moving and rather pathetic. The beautifully smooth, rounded form is just asking to be gripped.

80 This 'poppy' bench-end motif from Lincoln Cathedral illustrates the Bible story of Samson and Delilah. The three figures fit beautifully into the characteristic shape, and the overall design has been well-considered. The expression on the face of Delilah, and the 'tension' of Samson's body say much about the ability of the carver.

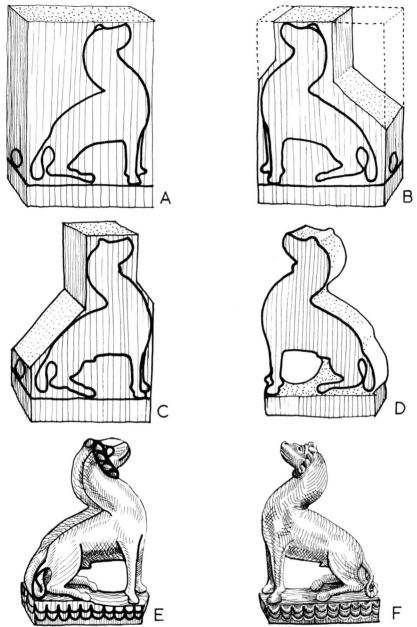

81 (A) For a simple three-dimensional subject, (in this case a hound), choose a block of straight-grained soft wood, and draw the hound on one side. (B) With a tenon saw cut away the wood, so that the hound fits the area that is left. (C) With a bow or keyhole saw, cut much closer to the subject. As the hound is symmetrical the original drawing may now be transferred to the other side of the wood. (D) At this stage it is essential that the block of wood is either held in a pair of carver's chops, or secured by one of the many patent holdfasts that are on the market. Now, using the keyhole or flexible saw, cut right up to the drawing. (E) Using one of the shallow spade gouges, or a front bent tool, shave off all the angles and corners – don't attempt to remove large single pieces of wood. (F) When the subject 'appears' there is always the possibility that the wood is badly grained, so you must be ready to improvise and adapt the original design.

69

illustrations it is necessary to choose a block of wood which is large enough to contain the object that you are going to carve. You would be well advised to choose a wood that is hard, free from knots and straight-grained. I suggest a light oak, as it is in character and within the spirit of the medieval experience.

It will make your task that much easier if the subject that you have chosen to carve is sitting good and solid on a base and with not too many extensions or projections. Fix the block of wood firmly to the bench – to grip it in the vice would be the best method as this does the least harm to the wood. The figure, or whatever, can now be drawn from all angles and on all sides of the block. It is good practice to make sure that you waste as little wood as possible. This means that your carving should fill out the block in the sense that the high points come near the surface of the wood.

You can now, using a coping or tenon saw, cut away the corners of the block, but don't be too rigid, always leave room for a change in design shape. Always be aware of the direction of the grain of the wood, otherwise if you short-grain your carving a piece might split off. You can now use a gouge to cut away waste wood, be sure to go over and over the whole carving – do not be tempted to concentrate on one small area.

As you proceed you must decide just how realistic or abstract your carving is going to be and you must also decide how it is going to be finished. This last problem is one which perhaps relates to the mental and artistic attitude that you have towards your work. Some carvers would say that a high sanded finish, one which obliterates all trace of tool marks, is desirable. For this particular carving, however, I would suggest that you consciously leave the marks of the tools on the surface of the wood. This is not an excuse for rough workmanship – you will need very sharp tools and I must emphasise you will have to keep referring to the direction of the grain. When you look at medieval carving you will see that at the time of carving the wood was finished well but without fuss. The patina that we now see has grown and is the result of three or four hundred years of

greasy palms and the rubbing of clothes. If you look closely underneath misericords at the areas that are visible but haven't been constantly rubbed, you will notice that the marks left by the sharp chisels and gouges can still be clearly seen.

When you have finished your carving, I would advise against a plastic lacquer – it would perhaps be more suitable if the wood was oiled or waxed. It would be impossible for me to describe all the problems that you might come across in the carving, but some general advice – don't design a piece of work that is too fussy, make the subject as solid as possible, work within your ability and be aware of your limitations.

Late Medieval and Early Renaissance Wood Carving

There was very little difference between church and domestic carving during this period, but the emphasis in both cases was on heavy solid oak chairs, benches, tables and chests. A poor man had very few possessions of any kind so our only terms of reference are the surviving items of carving from furniture, and the structural timbers from rich houses. The domestic buildings were timber-framed with plaster or brick filling between the timbers. The interiors of these large halls and houses are by modern standards bleak and massive, the only visual relief being the 'linenfold' carved wooden panelling, and the huge items of carved furniture placed around the sides of the room.

LINENFOLD PANELS
This type of carved motif is so common that it deserves a special mention. The pattern or design is as the name indicates a carved representation of vertically folded or pleated linen. The style it is thought, originated in France, and is perhaps an offshoot of the folded linen altar surrounds that were so popular in the early fourteenth century.

The basic design is nearly always the same and achieved in the same manner – a panel of wood is planed around the edges so that the background is slightly lower – now with a moulding plane, vertical hollows and rounds are cut, and finally the ends of the

82 A linenfold, panelled interior of a fifteenth
century house. The houses of rich merchants of
this period were, by modern standards, stark and
sparsely furnished. Furniture was limited to
huge chests, tables and massive bench seats – all
of which were heavily carved. The room interiors
were lined with wooden panels and these in turn
were covered by tapestries and hangings. Notice
the adjustable bench back – it can be swung over
so the user can sit on either side.

(*opposite*)
83   This medieval door post capital once stood outside 'King John's Palace', Nottingham, England, and is believed to date back to about 1600. It is massive, barbaric and very powerful – the figure totally fills the bracketed area, and was obviously intended to be structural as well as decorative (*Nottingham Castle Museum*).

(*right*)
84   Detail from 'King John's Palace', Nottingham, England. Carved on oak and in shallow relief the bearded figure fills out the area between the square door frame and the arched door. Dated about 1600 (*Nottingham Castle Museum*).

rounds are hand carved so that they give the appearance of folded cloth or linen. On the early examples the hollows are shallow, and the carved work delicate and minimal. It must be remembered that these wooden panels were primarily used for house interiors, not because they were good to look at, but because they concealed dark, cold, damp walls, and protected tapestries and hangings from contact with them.

CARVED FURNITURE
During the fourteenth and fifteenth centuries many new items of furniture were developed, so consequently carving as a form of domestic decoration became popular. In the medieval period life was so uncertain

that it was only possible to possess as much as you could personally safeguard. These uncertain conditions limited the type and style of the furniture, to the extent that the chief items were the bench, the chest, the bed, a combined chest chair and huge tables. These were mostly carved with linenfold or Gothic tracery motifs, and it is these which form the characteristic carvings of the period. The exterior carvings were limited mainly to massive crude door surrounds and repeated pattern carving on lintels and wall timbers. Nearly all the carvings of this period were inspired by the church stone and wood interiors, so the designs tended to be either shallow chip-carved circular motifs, which obviously drew their inspira-

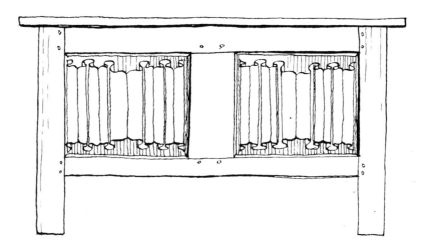

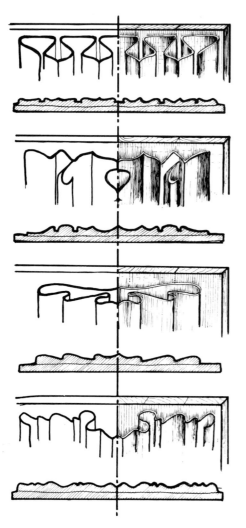

85 A real understanding and development of furniture as we now know it was marked by the introduction of 'framed' work. Boxes were framed up using tenon joints and grooved rails – the space in between being filled with thin boards which were often decorated with carved linenfold designs. The chest illustrated is early sixteenth century.

86 Various linenfold designs, and their cross sections.

87 French carved oak chest about 1480. The Gothic pierced tracery designs have been inspired by church work of the period. English carved work of the same date tended to be plainer and less 'architectural' (*Victoria and Albert Museum, London*).

tion from cathedral windows, or carved and pierced arched tracery which was inspired by church arcades and screens.

As the medieval period gave way to the influence of the Renaissance, oak had been so heavily used that it was in short supply. This shortage of a traditional material led the wood workers of the sixteenth century to experiment with new woods and new forms of furniture construction. The heavy plank construction of the furniture changed gradually to jointed and panelled structures which were not only lighter in weight, but were more economical in their use of timber. Gradually, building designs relied less on function and structure, and more on artistic and fashionable ornamentation. The carving techniques of this period became more lavish, and experimented with such innovations as 'turning' and wood inlay. The main motifs so far as the carver was concerned were strap work, fat turned and carved posts, masks and repeated foliage. Most of the carving was in low relief.

(above)

88 Strapwork – large chest, Quenby Hall, Leicestershire. The motifs shown are characteristic of the shallow carved work of the early seventeenth century. The wide flat lines which flow round the design mark the original surface of the wood, and all the rest of the design has been cut at a lower level.

(right)

89 Shallow chip-carved design motif from a mid-seventeenth century chest – typical of the period, when carving tended to be worked in low relief or incised. The actual motif shape looks very much like North European carved work.

90 English carved oak dresser dated 1659 with
the words – 'Repent the Lord is at hand, Watch
and Pray, Live well and Die well'. The carved
motifs are simple, but have a real charm – figures
of similar humour and liveliness can be seen on
the Thomas Toft slipware dishes of the 1670's
(*Victoria and Albert Museum, London*).

91 This Norwegian armchair of about the fifteenth century is pleasantly open in design, relying on turned posts rather than massiveness. The chip-carved designs, the 'roses', the 'twists' and the zigzags are very shallow, hardly more than incisions.

LINENFOLD PANEL CARVING

To carve a panel of this type is not in itself very complicated, but it does require a certain amount of carpentry knowledge, or at least a friend who is a carpenter. You will need a panel of a good hard wood which is about 3 cm thick, about 30 cm across the grain and about 60 cm long – this slab of wood also needs to be straight-grained and free from knots.

Now for your knowledge of carpentry, or the help a friend: a margin about 6 cm wide and about half the thickness of the wood is planed out round the edges of the panel. The panel is now grooved, and then ploughed out with a moulding plane. The precise number of hollows and rounds will of course depend on the exact design that you intend to carve – it might help if you now

92 An early seventeenth century chair –
thought to be Welsh. Although this chair has
motifs which are similar to those on the Norwegian chair it is heavier and rather stolid. The
'knotted serpents' design can be found on carvings which originate from places as far apart as
Romania, Norway, Russia, England and even
India.

refer to the illustrations. The depth of these
undulations will also depend on the design
of the end folds, but don't take the depth of
the hollows any lower than the margin of low
ground round the edge of the panel.

Once you have worked out the precise
shape of the end folds, and this shape has
been transferred to the wood, the cutting
can begin. Noting carefully the varying
depths of the folds, the chisel (or gouge,
depending on the shape) is pushed straight
down into the wood. You will see that the
wood crumbles away to the depth of the
margin ground. It is at this stage that you
must make constant reference to your
master drawing. When the end folds have
been 'cut in', you will have slightly to undercut the end folds so as to give an illusion of
depth. I would suggest that for the first

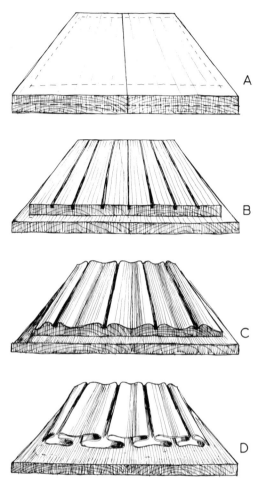

93 (A) A panel of wood about 3 cm thick, 30 cm wide and 60 cm long is prepared and marked up – it is important that the wood is straight-grained and free from knots. (B) A margin 6 cm wide is marked out on the panel, and using a rebate plane the surface of the wood is lowered until about half the thickness of the panel remains. Preliminary grooves are now cut which mark the depth of the undulations; this can be done with a circular saw or a hand plough. (C) Using a selection of round moulding planes the hollows are cut – the rounds are cut with the rebate plane. (D) The end folds are now cut with the shaped chisels and gouges.

attempt at linenfold carving you try on a piece of scrap wood until you appreciate the various depths of the folds. Don't be tempted to make the end shapes too complicated and also make constant references to your master drawings.

SHALLOW RELIEF CARVING

Carving of this character can be seen on both church and domestic furniture of the Gothic and Jacobean period. The carving is nearly always in low relief with the background wood cut away. Commonly used woods were oak, lime and pine.

Choose a good sound knot-free piece of timber that is at least 4–5 cm thick. I have chosen a piece of straight-grained pine. The wood is best fixed to the bench with a couple of clamps – in the illustration I've used a clamp and a screwed block – you could, if you were short of equipment, screw the wood straight onto the bench. Draw the design out in pencil, and colour with thin water paint the areas of the design that are to be cut away.

Using the veiner tool held firmly in the left hand and guided with the right, cut a shallow groove which follows the outline of the design. Now with one of the narrow chisels cut straight down into the grooved outline pressing the tool down to the full depth of the ground – say about 1 cm.

Using one of the shallow gouges cut out the ground or the painted area – cut across the grain as much as possible, not with it. When all the ground has been cut away to a depth of about 2 cm, clean out the sides of the motif using a medium gouge, so that the sides of the design gently curve into the ground.

If you can buy a piece of secondhand furniture at a sale or auction, carved repeats of this character can, with very little trouble, be cut into drawer or door fronts.

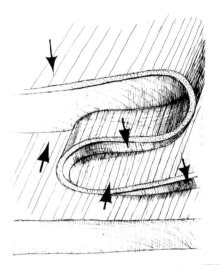

(*left*)
94   This detail illustrates how the end folds are to be cut; the arrows indicate the direction of the cuts.

(*below*)
95   (A) The wood, which in this case is about 5 cm thick, is fixed, clamped or screwed so that it is firm. The design is drawn out, and the areas that are to be removed are marked in with a thin water paint. (B) The main lines of the design are cut out; this is best done with a veiner tool. (C) Using the shaped gouges, the background or painted area is now cut away to a depth of about 2 cm. The surface design should curve gently into the cut away 'ground'.

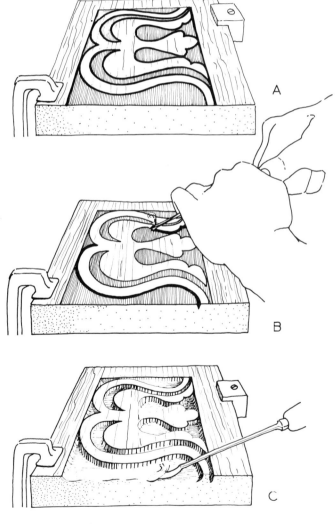

A

B

C

4

BUILT-UP, DRILLED AND PIERCED WORK

As the Renaissance developed, the naive style of the Gothic carvers was rejected and replaced by the naturalistic and decorated – realism became the order of the day. 'Modern' man had arrived, and he demanded large, exuberant and florid carvings on just about everything. In this new age the carver was equal to the task – plenty of wood from abroad – superb tools – a scien-

tific understanding of glues and stresses and above all the rich and famous queuing up with their commissions. The carver no longer worked in a solitary workshop at an easy pace, the work was highly organised on an almost production-line basis.

Of the many brilliant carvers of this period Grinling Gibbons is the one who must be mentioned, if for no other reason

96 (*top*) Carved swag from Windsor Castle – Grinling Gibbons.
(*left*) Drops, chestnuts and blackberries, from St Paul's Cathedral, carved by Jonathan Maine.
(*above*) Lime wood panel from Windsor Castle – Grinling Gibbons.

than the incredible amount of work that he produced. What the man in the street admires about Grinling Gibbons' carving is that it is so close to nature. Gibbons was born at just the period in history when his desire for realism in carving corresponded with an architectural demand for realism in interior decoration. He carved birds, fruit, feathers, flowers, shells, angels, etc, with such attention to detail that I find it is almost overwhelming. I could find fault with his attitude towards the subjects he carved, but his method and technique are faultless.

(*left*)
97 A portrait of the mature and successful Gibbons by Sir Godfrey Kneller.

(*below*)
98 Detail of a lime wood fragment from the chapel, Belton House, Lincolnshire. Most of Gibbons' work and 'Gibbons type' work was assembled from pinned and glued pieces; this particular sprig has split and come away from the main work.

Grinling Gibbons was born in 1648 in Holland, of an English father and a Dutch mother, so I think it fair to suggest that when he came to England to carve he was able to do so without being influenced by the heavy, beautiful and direct style of the English Gothic. He was about twenty when he was discovered by John Evelyn, the diarist. He was, as Evelyn said, 'working in an obscure place . . . a poor solitary thatched cottage', but before the month was out his work had been seen by the King, by Wren and by Pepys – Grinling Gibbons was well and truly launched. Gradually rich commissions came in and Gibbons had more work than he alone could manage. It was quite common for craftsmen of the period to have a team of apprentices who helped with the work but received little or no credit. Very soon Gibbons had established himself in a large workshop, and was in royal favour. When a commission was accepted and the

83

(right)
99 Charles II loved to wear point lace cravats, and Grinling Gibbons declared that he could carve one that was indistinguishable from the real thing. This beautiful example, which is now in the Victoria and Albert Museum, is from a cravat worn at a reception by Horace Walpole.

(below)
100 Lime wood carved fruit and flowers from the chapel, Belton House, Lincolnshire. This carving is mounted on a cedar panelled wall and, as you can see from the photograph, the carving is extraordinarily complex. This photograph which has been taken from the side, shows the depth of the carving, which in places is 12 cm deep.

design agreed upon, detailed sketches were set out and clay models made. This fine attention to detail is perhaps the chief characteristic of a Gibbons carving.

By this time, Gibbons had so many commissions that it is questionable just how much of the carving he actually did himself – but enough to say that everything that left his workshop was to a high standard. Gibbon was favoured by Charles II, James II and William and Mary: this in itself was amazing, the more so because they represented such religious and fashion extremes. Dutch William made Gibbons 'Chief of Works', and so far as Gibbons the wood carver is concerned this is where he begins his decline. By about 1696 Gibbons had begun to carve in stone, and his style became so very large and showy that it borders on being vulgar.

Grinling Gibbons worked mainly in lime wood which he glued, built up, undercut

and laminated. Lime is yellowish-white in colour, very close-grained, relatively free from knots, and cuts evenly in almost any direction. The wood in fact was perfect for Gibbons – his style of carving required a wood that he could totally dominate – he was not interested in a material that had character or figuring.

The fashionable desire for realism and deep relief led to the technique known as built-up, pinned or glued work. This means that parts of the carving that project are built up from many smaller pieces of wood glued and pinned together. This method of carving is tricky and in most cases not entirely necessary. It does become valid however if the 'span' of the subject to be carved cannot be cut from one solid lump of wood. With many Gibbons designs it was often the case that a wing, or an angel, or whatever, projected so far out of relief that it was carved as a separate piece and then pinned on at a later stage. This method of carving calls for very detailed drawings of the overall design and a total preconception of the finished work – so it is often beyond the ability of today's average carver.

Examples of Grinling Gibbons' carving can be found in many of the large stately homes and it is in these that you can study his technique and style.

Many of his carvings which are built up of layers of lime wood reach a depth that in certain cases exceeds 30 cm. Lime, if kept in dry conditions, is reasonably stable, and it is

101 Detail from a carved overmantle, Burghley House, England. In many cases the wings of Grinling Gibbons' birds were designed to be joined on in the final stages of the work, which I believe is the case in this 'doves group'.

(opposite)
102   Belton House, Lincolnshire. This detail from a carving over the fireplace bears the so-called 'Gibbons peapod' thought by many to be the trade mark of Gibbons – but this particular carving is the work of Edmund Carpenter. There is documentation to prove that in 1688 Sir John Brownlow paid Edmund Carpenter £25.

(above)
103   Part of a shell garland entwined with pearl ropes – Grinling Gibbons 1680. This detail comes from the so called Cosimo panel, a spectacular carving which was sent by Charles II to Cosimo III, Grand Duke of Tuscany, and is considered by many to be Grinling Gibbons' masterpiece.

(right)
104   Cherubim winged heads on a pierced screen, Trinity College, Oxford. On a lot of Grinling Gibbons' later work, detached winged heads began to dominate the designs – by this time in his career, a lot of 'his' work would have been actually carved by juniors and apprentices.

105 This detail from Belton House, Lincoln-shire, was carved by Edmund Carpenter – it is a real beauty, and is unlike the podgy, paunchy cherubs of Gibbons. This particular cherub is part of a group which is scrambling up one panel and down the next. Note – the little wings have been carved separately and stuck on at a later stage.

106 Miles and miles of moulding were carved in the seventeenth century, and although rep-etitious, it calls for a steady hand and sharp tools. Wood was shaped with moulding planes, then the surface of the moulding was marked out in a grid and carved. If moulding designs are analysed it can be seen that the repeated cuts are usually relatively simple.

this we have to thank for the good condition of Gibbons' work. Gibbons also worked in oak, but as this is a wood which does not take kindly to being built up and glued, he then usually worked within the limitations of the size of single pieces of wood. When however he did build up in unsuitable woods his carv-ings have begun to split and drift apart. Although certain carving tools are now referred to as 'Gibbons gouges' or 'a Gibbons', the marks left by the tools can rarely be seen on his work. It is this excessive attention to a high, perfect, smooth finish that is the main characteristic of late six-teenth and seventeenth century wood carving. Many of the carvings were de-signed to be gilded or painted, and it is this which above all tells us that wood was used primarily for decoration, and it just hap-pened to be the most available material. In his time Gibbons must have carved miles of door and window mouldings and, as gradu-ally the craft degenerated, it became a way of mass-producing pattern for pattern's sake. Plaster replaced wood as a means of pattern-ing building interiors and so, in the eight-eenth and nineteenth centuries, carvers began to concentrate almost wholly on carved furniture.

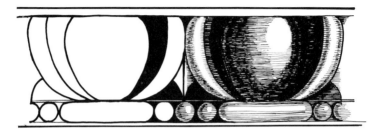

107 Characteristic carved mouldings of the
seventeenth century.

Preparation of Built-up Work

Often there is some confusion between
undercut, built-up and pegged work, so I
will describe each method.

UNDERCUT

Undercut refers to carving which has been
worked from one solid block of wood. The
carving is usually in the form of a deep relief
which has been so cut away that it is almost
free from its background. Many of the
Gothic misericord seats were so undercut
that it is possible to poke a finger under and
round the carved figures. The advantage of
this type of technique is that it gives the
carving an aesthetic quality that cannot be
obtained in any other way. There is also considerable pleasure in the knowledge that the
carving, because of its complications, is a
special expression of personal accomplish-

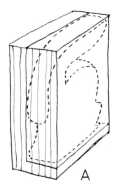 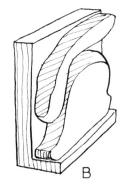 

A　　　　　B　　　　　C

108 (A) With this simple undercut carving, the design is marked out on one side of the wood only. (B) The design is cut out with a gouge, until the subject has been worked through to the 'ground'. (C) With a finished piece of undercut work, the subject should give the illusion that it is only lightly attached to its background. For this type of work you will need a goodish selection of small bent and shaped gouges.

ment. Of course undercutting is slow and expensive in labour and materials, but often it is the only way to achieve one's aim. It has been said that undercutting, because of the problems involved, can be considered to be the wood carver's *tour de force*.

GLUED AND PEGGED WORK
The carvers of the Renaissance were so swayed by fashion and style that they had to spend most of their time working against the natural inclination of the wood. The designs of the period called for such physical depth, breadth and realistic three-dimensionalism that there was really no alternative to building up and laminating the wood. Grinling Gibbons and most of the other carvers of the period built up, glued, pegged and 'planted' separate carved lumps on a base and in this way created startling illusions of reality. The only thing against this type of approach to carving is that it requires considerable mechanical skill, an understanding of wood stresses and glues, and a feeling for piecemeal composition.

Glued work here means single carvings which because of their depth and dimensions require to be carved out of one lump that is a lamination of several separate pieces of wood. If you want to carve a free figure it might be as well first to search for an irregular branch, bough or root that will contain your design. If this isn't possible then you will have to consider glueing several pieces of wood together – this shouldn't be attempted until you have a basic understanding of the properties of your materials. Certain woods don't 'take', and the glue either just doesn't work, or cracks and distorts the

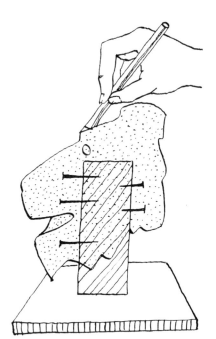

109 Before a large and detailed work is started, a scaled down model should be made – nothing elaborate, just an armature and plasticine will suffice.

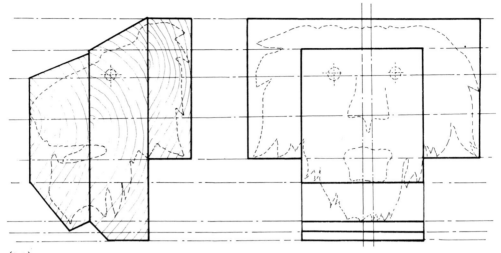

(*top*)
110   Built-up work is economical on materials
and labour as the shape of the glued up blocks can
approximate the planned carving. It is important
that you use wood that is straight-grained and
free from knots.

111   As you can see from this illustration, the
finished carving 'fills' the available wood – there
is no point in gluing up vast amounts of material if
you are then going to cut most of it away. The
design stages of built-up work are critical, and
require considerable thought and planning.

carving, so it is vital that before you undertake such work you research your materials. One way of finding out if a particular wood is suitable for your purpose is to go to museums and see which woods the carvers of the past used. In all cases it is extremely important that the wood is well-seasoned and stable. Grinling Gibbons used lime and pear wood, but there are many others such as box, cedar, laburnum, mahogany, yew, so contact a good, high-class timber merchant and see what he has in stock.

When you have designed your carving, made a small model out of, say, plasticine or clay, obtained the full-size measurements, decided on the type of wood and chosen the type of glue, then you are ready to start work.

A point about glue – there are now hundreds of glues on the market and they all have different uses and qualities, but I suggest that a white PVA glue, obtainable from most wood merchants, is the best.

When designing the carving, you will have to consider which way you want the grain to run, because after all this is going to affect the 'building up' – the grain of the joined-on section of wood will have to be considered also. If possible the grain of the added timber should run in the same direction as the main timber; in this way you will obtain maximum strength from the glue. If you can, avoid joining two different timber types or joining end-grain to end-grain. The surfaces to be glued together should be smooth and free from dust, moisture and dirt. The glue should be worked into both surfaces until the fibres of the wood are saturated. There is no benefit to be obtained if you have glue oozing out all over the place – just the opposite in fact, it is wasteful, messy and decreases bond efficiency. Of course, before you do any of this you must consider just how the work is to be clamped up. For a small piece, a couple of G clamps might be sufficient, otherwise you might have to use larger extending clamps, or one of the patent strap clamps that are now obtainable. Once the wood has been glued and built up, you can carve, using one of the techniques already discussed.

Drilled and Pierced Patterns
and
Eighteenth Century Furniture

In the eighteenth century the fashions of the period were perfectly suited for the art of the carver. New woods such as satin, from the West Indies, India and Ceylon, ebony from Africa, mahogany from South America, rosewood from Brazil and many other exotics were being regularly imported into this country. These new materials, plus easier travel and cheap printing, brought wider influences on furniture and decorative tastes, which were no longer necessarily related to domestic traditions. The carving of this period was mainly on furniture, which drew its inspiration from India, China, Africa and European Romantic Classic. The furniture and interiors became sculptural as well as functional, designers being concerned with total environment. The age was prosperous and England was the centre of the political and artistic world. Of course the styles and designs became excessive and florid, but it was, for the carver and worker in wood, a opportunity for experimentation and recognition. A social revolution was taking place, carvers were no longer illiterate and unknown workers – a new type of craftsman was emerging. For the first time in the history of carving and furniture design, the carver/designer was publishing books and manuals which illustrated his work. Four furniture designer/carvers of this period dominated the style of carving of the eighteenth and nineteenth centuries.

THOMAS CHIPPENDALE 1718–1779
Chippendale, the son of a Yorkshire carpenter, is the best-known of the English chair makers of this period. In 1754 he published *The Gentlemen and Cabinet-Makers Directory*, intended for workshops and wealthy people who wanted their furniture to be in fashion. The book contained illustrations, designs and instructions for almost every type of domestic furniture – but the emphasis was on rococo pierced-back chairs made in mahogany. The 'Chippendale style' became so widespread that his personal

112 A late seventeenth century chair, with
turned supports, cherubs and scroll patterns,
Belton House, Lincolnshire. Chairs of this
character, with their pierced and carved backs,
strongly influenced the development and design
of chairs made in the eighteenth century.

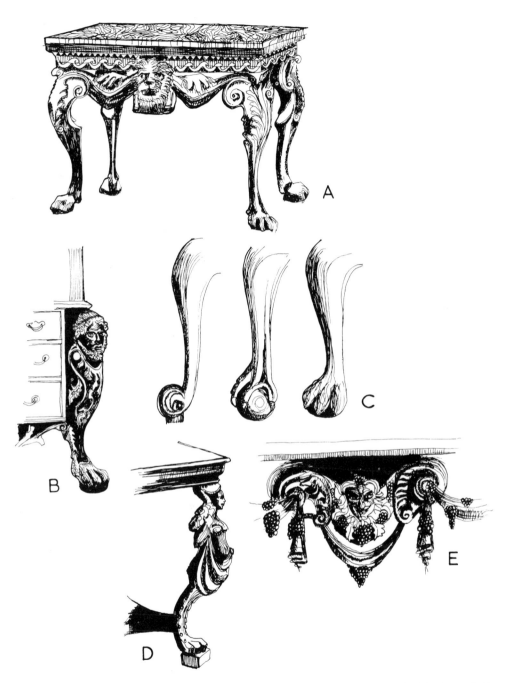

113 (A) Characteristic cabriole legs of the middle of the eighteenth century. (B) Classical mask and animal leg, of cabinet, 1745. (C) Three types of chair legs – scroll, claw and paw. (D) A 'combination' female bust and animal leg, from a silver gilt table, 1670. (E) Mask and swags from a mahogany table, 1730.

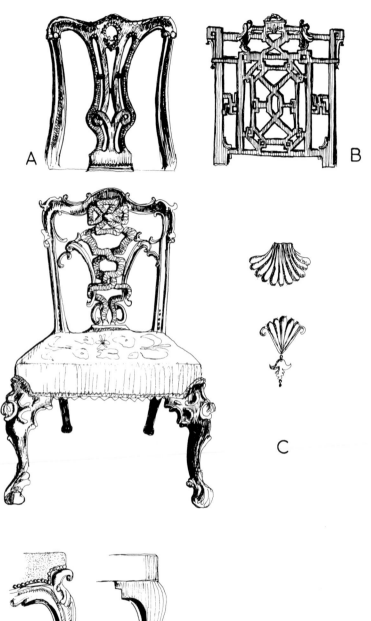

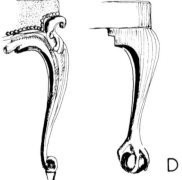

114 Characteristic Chippendale chair designs 1718–79. (A) Design for Chippendale chair back. (B) A design influenced by Chinese fretwork. (C) This 'ribbanded' chair, with the carved shells on the legs and splats, was one of Chippendale's most popular designs, 1755. (D) Simplified chair leg designs of the 1760's.

115　This carved chair – English, 1760, with its
strapwork, fretted stretchers and pierced back,
has about it a firmness of shape and design that
mark it as Chippendale (*Victoria and Albert
Museum, London*).

117 Robert Adam approached the problem of furniture design from an architectural viewpoint; this piece of furniture looks more like a Greek temple than a table. The detail of the carving is very fine, and the delicacy of the piercing is amazing.

work is difficult to identify. The main characteristic is the variety of design of the pierced chair backs and the strength and solidity of their construction. His designs are heavily influenced by Gothic and Eastern pattern forms and this is most in evidence in the carved masks and animal-related feet on his table and chair legs.

ROBERT ADAM 1728–1792
Adam was born in Scotland and studied under his father, a famous architect of the period, but completed his education in Rome, Florence and Venice. Within a very short time he became established as an architect and designer, his influence spreading throughout all the applied arts of the eighteenth and nineteenth centuries, and up to the present day. Obviously his style was a direct interpretation of the classic designs he had seen on his travels; his furniture designs are heavy with swags, columns, capitals and fluting.

GEORGE HEPPLEWHITE d1786
Very little is known about Hepplewhite except that he was apprenticed to a Robert Gillow of Lancaster. In 1788, two years after Hepplewhite's death, his widow published *The Cabinet Maker and Upholsterers Guide*, which had three separate editions. It contains over three hundred

(opposite)
116 This grand exhibition piece, carved by A. Barbaretti, Siena, was shown at the 1851 exhibition. It has in its design all the carved clichés which Robert Adam managed to pick up on his grand Mediterranean tour, eg classical figures, fluted columns, animal friezes (*Victoria and Albert Museum, London*).

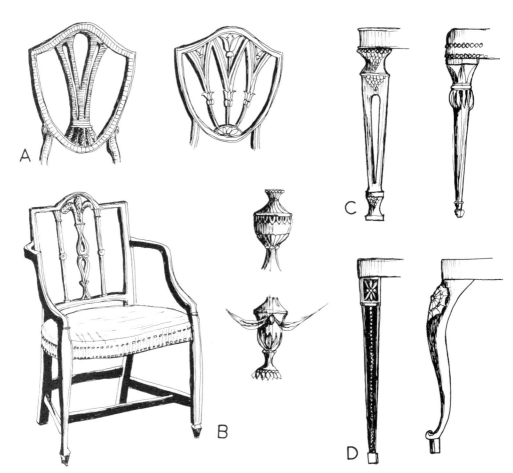

118 Designs taken from the 3rd edition of Hepplewhite's book, *The Cabinet Makers and Upholsterers Guide*, 1749. (A) Delicate chair back
design that typifies the sensitivity of the Hepplewhite style. (B) The urn, urn and swags, and the
three feathers were much used Hepplewhite
chair back splat motifs; note the squaring of the
chair backs. (C) Designs for straight chair legs.
(D) Designs for stool legs.

(*opposite*)
119 Carved chair 1775, mahogany, English.
The motifs on this particular chair relate very
much to church carving of early periods. At the
same time work of this type must also have
influenced the Art Nouveau carvers of the early
twentieth century (*Victoria and Albert Museum,
London*).

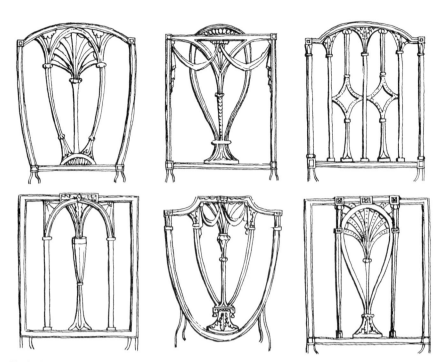

120 Chair back designs taken from Thomas Sheraton's book, *The Cabinet Makers and Upholsterers Drawing Book*, 1793. Sheraton chairs are noted for delicate ornamentation, fluting, reeding, and beautiful inlays. It is thought by many that his designs mark the climax of carved English furniture. His designs were still being used through the nineteenth century.

designs, which on the whole are extensions of the work of Adam and Chippendale. The chairs however showed a development of style which is expressed in the use of satin wood, carved smooth curves, graceful carved pierced backs and carved motifs such as urns, chains and feathers.

THOMAS SHERATON 1751–1806
Sheraton was the son of a cabinet maker, and it is on record that he himself worked for many years in the trade. He made a living by teaching drawing and selling drawing-books. About 1793 he published a work called *The Cabinet Maker and Upholsterers Drawing Book*. This was not only a collection of his own designs, but also a description of furniture being made at that time. It is thought that Sheraton at some time must have been a carver because his drawings show that he understood the technique of wood carving, and wherever possible his designs included carved motifs. When a piece of furniture is described as Sheraton, it means that it relates to designs that can be seen in his book. The backs of Sheraton chairs tend to be delicate, slender, squarish and highly carved.

Although these four men were not wood

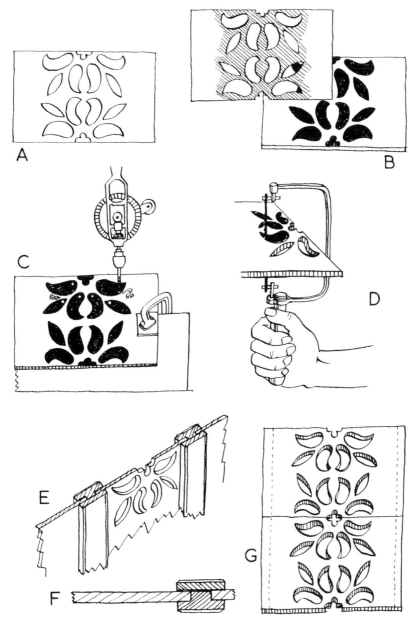

121 (A) Draw out the design and cut out a
stencil. (B) Stencil the design through onto the
prepared board. (C) Each area that is to be cut
away must have a drilled starting hole, through
which the saw blade can be passed. (D) Using a
fret or coping saw, the stencilled areas are
removed. (E) The boards are cleaned up and
slotted into a grooved wooden frame. (F) A cross
section, showing construction. (G) It is important that the design is fully considered before you
start – in this way the motifs can be linked.

103

carvers, their influence must have been felt by most of the town and country carvers of the period. Their span of authority spread over most of the eighteenth century, and well into the nineteenth. The carved embellishments on the furniture reached such a peak of ornateness that the only direction that carvers and designers could take was 'down'. The designs gradually changed and evolved until they became streamlined and functionalised, so that it could be said that these four designers are partly responsible for the lack of carving on late nineteenth-century work. The carvers of the Victorian age became obsessed with reproduction and massiveness to the exclusion of originality. There are exceptions to this, but they will be dealt with in the next chapter.

A Grille or Room-Divider Screen

With this method of carving it is very important that you work out your design beforehand. You will be removing large areas of wood with either a fret-type saw or a drill, or both, and unless you work to full planned design there is a danger that the piece of wood will collapse.

As a general rule I suggest that the proportion of cut-away wood is no more than half the total and that the main structure of the pattern or design follows the direction of the grain. Next problem is the type of wood to use, its thickness and its use. If the carving is intended for decoration, say for a picture frame or some such, then you can cut away just about as much as you dare. If on the other hand the carving is in some way to be structural and under stress, then start with a piece of wood at least 3 cm thick.

The technique involves drilling out the pattern, cleaning up the edges with a flexible blade saw, and then finally carving the design in more detail. With this technique the final design will depend very much on the character of the wood. The Gothic carvers used oak, but then it was very thick so there was little danger of it breaking on short-grained areas. The eighteenth-century chair carvers used mahogany – this cuts and carves well, but on short-grained sections it tends to be brittle. Box wood and lime work well; they can be expensive, but they will give you more freedom for experimentation and fine design. If the wood is close-grained it will allow you to have long continuous lines and parts of the design almost free from connection.

The character of the design which you want to create will relate to the type of tools used. You can either let the composition of the design reflect the action of the tool, as can be seen in the drilled pattern illustration, or you can anticipate and design around the known result of the tools.

Draw the design onto tracing paper, and with masking tape fix the design firmly to the piece of wood to be carved. Using a fine craft knife remove the areas of the design that you are going to cut away. Now with a thin almost colourless water paint, stencil through the cut-away paper design; when the paint has dried take off the tracing paper stencil and put it to one side for reference. Fix the piece of wood to the bench with a clamp, making sure that there is a piece of scrap wood between your work and the bench, and drill holes through the areas of the wood that you want to remove.

A couple of points – I prefer to use a hand drill because it gives me more control, and I drill as large a hole as the design permits. Take the scrap wood away from under your work, and move it to the side of the bench so that the areas to be cut away hang over the bench edge. Using a fine coping saw, and for this you will have to pass the saw blade through your design and then fix it to your saw, cut round the edges of your design. It is important that the saw is held upright, otherwise you will be cutting at an angle through the thickness of the wood, and the work will be spoilt. When you have reached this stage, the wood can be clamped back on the bench and the design gouged or worked as explained in other chapters.

5

TURNED WORK, FURNITURE
AND DOMESTIC WARE

Wood turning is the craft of shaping wood into round or oval sections by means of a lathe. This method of shaping wood is very ancient and is referred to in old writings and records: Pliny mentions 'Thericles who was famous for his skill at wood turning'. Without the lathe much of the worked and carved wood that we now take for granted would not have been possible. The turners of wood really only came into their own in the fifteenth, sixteenth and seventeenth centuries when it became fashionable to have beds with massive turned and carved posts, chairs with turned legs and backs and tables with bulbous turned and carved central legs. Before I tell you why it was done, it would perhaps be better to tell you how it was done.

Simple Lathes

In operation the wood to be turned is made to revolve at speed on a horizontal axis – the revolving surface of the wood is then cut by means of hand-held gouges and chisels. The turner rests his cutting tools on a bar, then pushes the cutting edges against the spinning wood, which removes the corners and angles. Gradually the wood is reduced to a section which is circular or oval.

There are now many types of lathes, but as far as we are concerned the early 'powered' lathes are of primary interest. The lathes used by seventeenth-century turners were generally wooden, and of simple construction. They were known as pole and bow lathes. Both these consist of a bed or table, with two stout vertical posts or 'puppets' (sometimes called 'poppets') fixed up

through it. One of the 'puppets' carries an iron pin, while the other has an adjustable screw or handle. Both the pin and the screw have points which grip the work and hold it securely. The support for the tools is a horizontal bar which goes from one 'puppet' to the other.

With the pole lathe, the work is turned by means of a foot treadle – a cord is fixed to the treadle, passes several times round the wood that is to be turned, and is then fixed to the end of a springy pole. In use the turner moves the treadle with one foot, and at the same time pushes his cutting tool against the wood which is turning. When the treadle touches the ground he removes his foot and the spring action of the pole turns the wood in a backwards direction. So with this type of lathe the wood to be worked spins backwards and forwards, and can only be cut when being turned forwards.

For more delicate work a bow lathe was used. This is similar to the pole lathe, with the exception that the heavy sprung pole is replaced by a wooden bow. The cord that goes from the treadle and then round the work is then joined to the string of the bow.

The snag with both of these lathes is that as the work can only be cut when the treadle is being pushed down, there is some loss of efficiency. Nevertheless lathes of this simple type were used right through the Middle Ages, up until early this century. In the nineteenth century the continuous-direction lathe was developed and this was either operated by a wheel-turning assistant or a foot crank and treadle. Because it was so simple to use there was a great increase in the

105

122 (*top and left*) The head and turned supports from a seventeenth century bed, Berkeley Castle. (*below*) A panel from the foot of a bed, Jacobean, Quenby Hall, Leicestershire.

123 Medieval pole lathe, after a German manuscript, 1399. This type of early lathe was powered by the sprung pole, and the cord, but as you can see, the wood could only be worked on the downward movement of the foot.

output of turned legs for chairs and stools, turned kitchenware such as bowls and rollers and turned and carved toys.

The tools used by the turner are chisels, gouges, planes and knives. First the centres are found at each end of the wood that is to be turned, then with a plane – some of the rural turners use a hatchet – the corners of the wood are removed so that it is more or less rounded. The wood is then gripped at the centres between the two points of the lathe and roughed out with a large gouge. The gouge is held so that the cutting blade just skims the work – at no time should the gouge be forced at right angles into the wood. When the wood is roughly round in section the chisels are used – these long-handled double-bevelled-edge chisels are moved from side to side along the whole length of the work, until the dimensions and shape are as required. The wood is usually sanded, waxed and polished while still revolving on the lathe.

In Europe in the sixteenth and seventeenth centuries the development that was taking place in furniture making called for an increased number of turned legs, rods,

124   Using a nineteenth century treadle lathe. The left hand guides and supports the chisel, the right hand supplies the pressure (*Rutland County Museum*).

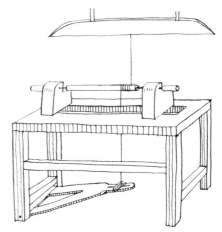

125   After an illustration in *Tomlinson's Cyclopaedia of Useful Arts and Manufactures Vol II*, about 1860. This bow lathe is worked on the same principal as the pole lathe, the main difference being that the power is more constant and perhaps less vigorous, so a lathe of this type was used only for delicate work.

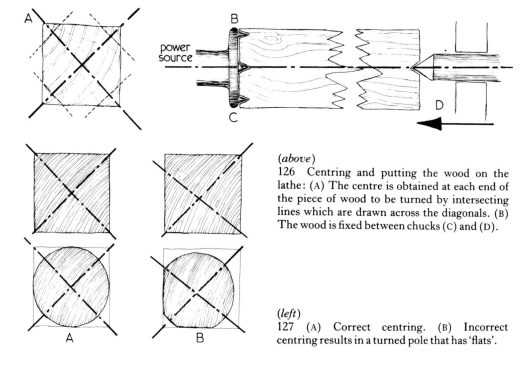

(*above*)
126 Centring and putting the wood on the lathe: (A) The centre is obtained at each end of the piece of wood to be turned by intersecting lines which are drawn across the diagonals. (B) The wood is fixed between chucks (C) and (D).

(*left*)
127 (A) Correct centring. (B) Incorrect centring results in a turned pole that has 'flats'.

spindles and bulbous poles and it was this, more than anything else, that really brought to the forefront the craft of wood turning.

Stately Home Furniture

Stately homes often contain good examples of domestic turned and carved furniture, for their owners bought the best available and the items have been in constant use. Of all the stately-home furniture, the four-poster bed is in its development, design and structure the most interesting.

So far as woodwork is concerned, beds don't really appear on the scene until about the sixteenth century. Before this date the beds of the wealthy were 'trussed' or 'trundle' camp-type beds, simple frames with rope or leather webbing. Poor people were lucky if they had a bunk cupboard or a bag of straw. The medieval grand houses were large, draughty and cold and as conditions became more stable and settled, and it was no longer important that furniture was portable and 'knock down', comfort replaced security as the most important factor in furniture design. Beds with more

style and a lot more comfort were required.

The first stage in making beds more comfortable was to fix a curtain to the ceiling so that it hung all round the bed; this did at least keep out some of the draught. As the ceilings were high it became the practice to supply the bed with its own cover, a false ceiling, usually fixed to the wall at the head of the bed and supported by two posts at the foot. The bed itself was completely independent of either curtain or posts. There are many variations on this curtains-and-posts theme – some beds had wooden walls and ceilings, some had little roofs or covers at the head of the bed, some had wooden posts and tent-like curtains and drapes.

After the sixteenth century the bed became the most important and prestigious item of furniture. At first the posts were square in section, but gradually they became more and more lavish, and more related to classical architectural pillars, plinths and columns. It is the scale of these posts that is so very interesting – it must be supposed that at first they were made from straight tree trunks. Later it became necessary for them to be prefabricated and constructed

128 Turned 'bobbin chair' – ash and oak,
English 1620 (*Victoria and Albert Museum,
London*).

(*above left*)
129   Early sixteenth century canopy bed, Switzerland. The wooden cantilevered canopy on this bed gave protection from draughts and leaky roofs. The flat carved motifs are similar to those found on Jacobean English work.

(*above right*)
130   Turned and carved bedposts. (A) Early sixteenth century. (B) Late sixteenth century. The beautiful turned and carved designs of this period seemed to best express themselves on bedposts – in some cases the carving completely obliterates the work of the turner.

(*left*)
131   Late sixteenth century bed. With these so-called 'four poster' beds the flat canopy was joined to the head of the bed, while it was supported at the foot by two posts which were entirely independent of the main bed structure. The turned posts with their massive bulges were made from glued-up blocks of wood which were built-up; this avoided waste wood, which at the time was in short supply.

132   A seventeenth century bed in the Pomegranate Room, Quenby Hall, Leicestershire.

133   A Tudor draw leaf table. The huge Tudor 'bulb' legs had to be built up by the turner; they gradually reached a stage in their design when the leg became all 'bulb', so that it looked almost as if the table was supported on four massive plum shapes.

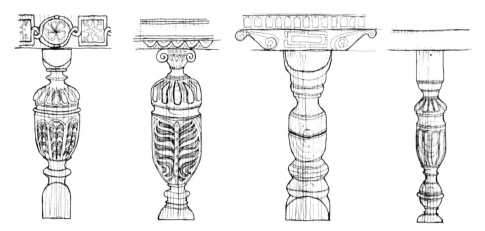

from a combination of glued and carved sections. For the turner of wood the legs and posts of huge beds must have presented quite a problem – just by their scale and massiveness they were technically a big undertaking. On close inspection it can be seen that most of the posts are built up, with a square pierced and carved plinth, a carved capital and a turned pillar. By the late sixteenth and early seventeenth century the turned part of the bed post was, more often than not, either made up from turned lumps threaded onto a central post, or made from a central spindle that was built and glued up to the rough shape and then turned. It is this development of economical usage of timber that marks the start of furniture as we now know it.

Through the carving and design of the furniture, whether posts for the beds, legs for the huge tables or legs for the chairs, there usually ran a pattern and structure theme. The characteristic feature of the turned furniture of the sixteenth, seventeenth and eighteenth centuries is the use of huge bulges in the turned uprights. Often these turnings have been so carved and worked that it is difficult to see that they were originally turned. These bulbous turned and carved features have been described as pomegranates, bulbs and lidded chalices. I think it fair to say that the beds and tables represent the best and the last of the really expressive turned and carved furniture. Of course, in the nineteenth century furniture was carved and worked, but it was so influenced by mass

134 Various turned table legs dated about 1600.

production and mechanisation that for the carver it ceases to be relevant.

Making a Large Turned Container

This is quite a big undertaking and you will need the use of a lathe with a distance between the poppets of at least 30 cm. For this project you will need six pieces of straight-grained pine that measure 4 cm thick, 12½ cm wide and 30 cm long. You will also need two discs of 'half-inch' ply with diameters of 16 cm and two hexagonal pieces of 'half-inch' ply with sides that measure 8 cm. Take a ply disc and glue to it one of the hexagonal pieces of ply – this is then repeated with the other disc. The pieces of pine are planed so that one side measures 12½ cm – the other sides are planed so that they angle in at 60°. If you have any problems at this point, refer to the diagrams. When the six pieces of wood are planed they should all have one side that measures 30 cm × 8 cm – it is this side that forms the inside of the container. The six sides are now glued and clamped together. Both discs are also glued so that the hexagonal faces are inside the container.

This 30 cm long hexagonal tube is now centred on the lathe and turned, until the radius measures 8 cm. By the time you reach this stage you should have a wooden tube with both ends closed. With the tube still on

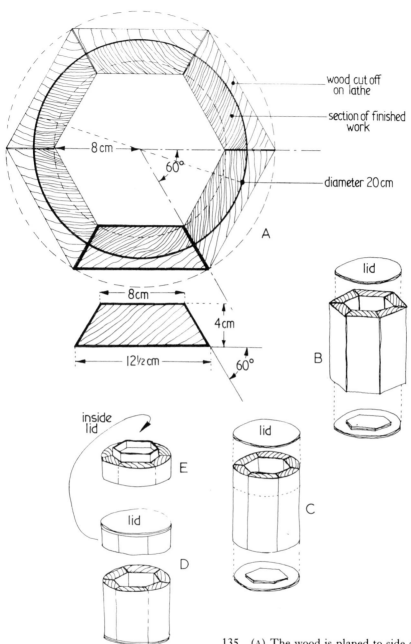

wood cut off
on lathe

section of finished
work

diameter 20 cm

8 cm

60°

A

8cm

4 cm

12½ cm

60°

lid

B

inside
lid

lid

E

lid

D

lid

C

135 (A) The wood is planed to side angles of 60° and then glued together – the best clamp for holding this type of work while the glue sets, is either a large 'jubilee' clip, or a dowel and twisted cord. (B) The ends are glued in place. (C) The hexagonal box is turned on the lathe until it is round in section, and the lid end is marked with a groove. (D) Using a fine saw the lid end is cut off. (E) Using thin bits of ply a projecting lip is glued to the inside of the lid.

113

the lathe, cut a groove about 7 cm from one end – this will mark the depth of the lid. Polish the container and take it from the lathe. With a fine saw cut through the tube at the point indicated by the groove. Using thin ply, glue a 3 cm projecting lip to the inside of the lid. This container relates in design and construction to the bed posts of the seventeenth and eighteenth centuries, also there are links with the tobacco and tea caddies that were so popular in the nineteenth century.

The method and design can be changed so that there are a greater number of sides, and the sides can be made from alternate dark and light woods.

Cottage Chairs

Most of the references made to the furniture of the past have been related to the furniture of rich merchants and nobles. The poor cottage dwellers had to make do with logs, benches and stools. At the end of the fifteenth century when conditions became more settled, the idea and use of chairs began to spread – at first just primitive three-legged stools, but gradually these were developed until they were three-legged with arms and a very primitive back-rest. During the sixteenth century chairs became more common and were financially within the reach of all but the desperately poor.

Cottage chairs as they were called, served the needs of the servants, farmers and inn keepers and the increased usage led to the setting up of a 'chair industry'. This industry developed in the then heavily wooded areas around Buckinghamshire, and especially the town of High Wycombe. Chairs of almost identical design were, at the same period, being made in North America. The American version developed into the 'Benjamin Franklin' rocking chair, which was more often than not painted green or red. The English cottage or Windsor chair has always been a unique product, made by two or three men, each of whom undertakes only one part. The essential difference between cottage chairs and other working-class functional chairs is that they are made from turned wood rather than

136 A characteristic Windsor chair with stick back construction and cresting bar – and designs for splats. It is very interesting to note that many of the fretted designs of the Windsor chair backs are simplified versions of the designs drawn up by Hepplewhite and Sheraton. The seats are usually made from thick timber slabs; it is the adzed 'dish' and the scooped front edge that give them an illusion of lightness.

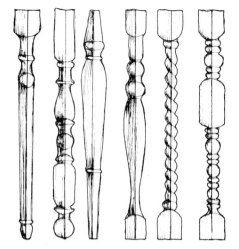

137   Various turned chair legs for cottage furniture.

Although all the different components of cottage chairs are hand-made and totally individual, it is the design of the backs that makes them so interesting. The chair backs are often plain rods set at intervals, but sometimes the space in the centre is filled with a pierced and carved splat. The variations of splat designs are many, but their method of construction is always the same. The splats are made from oak or walnut, they are pierced and cut with a fret-saw, and the edges are chamfered. The cottage, Windsor or wheel-back chairs are in my opinion the ideal culmination of the turner's and carver's craft experience, in that they are in proportion and scale, perfectly suited for their purpose. A good hand-made Windsor chair has in its seat, back, arms and legs, swellings and shapes that are so closely related to the human body that they appear to have evolved naturally.

squared wood, and they have, until recently, been a cottage or home industry.

CHAIR BODGER
Using unseasoned beech as his raw material, the chair bodger is the man who makes all the turned parts of the chair. Working in pairs, a bodger and his mate would set up a workshop in the woods and produce all the turned components. First the mate would cut short sections of wood, then he would split and quarter them. Working on a 'donkey' or 'horse', he sat and worked the quarters of wood until they were roughly round in section, and slightly tapered at each end. The chair bodger, using the traditional pole lathe, would then work the billets of wood into the legs and spars of the chair.

CHAIR MAKER
The chair-maker proper produced everything apart from the turned parts, and in many ways his craft function was nearer to that of a saddler or cooper than a furniture-maker. With this realisation comes the idea that the origins of cottage chairs are akin to those of carts, wheels and barrels. The seat is cut from a single slab of elm and shaped and carved with an adze until it has a shallow saddle-like depression. The legs are then banged into holes in the seat and wedged.

Making a Welsh Milking Stool

For this project you will need a slab of wood 30 cm wide × 30 cm long × 8 cm thick, and three turned legs about 30 cm long and about 5 cm thick. I have to assume that either you know how to turn wood on the lathe (so you won't need any help in this stage), or that you don't have access to a lathe, so have decided to purchase the legs.

Using a compass or whatever, draw a circle with a radius of 15 cm on your slab of wood – you would be advised to use elm, as this resists splitting and warping. Cut out the circle of wood with a bow or large coping saw, and then with it gripped in a vice, clean up the edges. The best tool for cutting a good rounded-section edge on the slab of wood is either a hollow draw knife, or a spoke shave; if you can't obtain either of these, then one of the very common open-tooth rasps will do.

You should now have a disc of wood which is 30 cm in diameter, and has rounded edges. With the compass set at a radius of 10 cm, mark out the disc of wood so that there is a 5 cm margin all round the circumference.

For the next step you will need to use a small adze or a shallow gouge – but with the disc secured, the centre of the wood has to be 'dished' or carved so that there is a

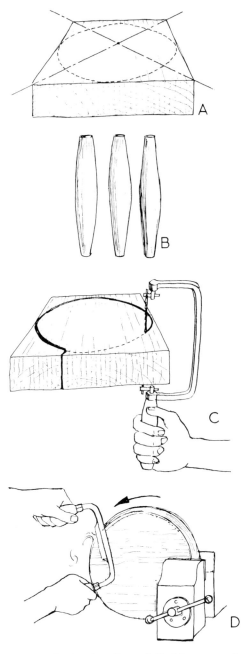

depression about 4 cm deep. This 'dishing' of the stool seat must be done with caution. Whenever possible cut across the grain – of course eventually you will have no choice but to cut in all directions, so keep your tools sharp and don't cut too deep. You will soon find that if you are using the tools incorrectly, the grain of the wood will resist and hamper your progress. If when you are cutting with the grain you force the gouge too deep, there is a danger that the wood will tear away in long splinters, so caution and restraint are vital.

When you are ready to set the legs in the seat, clamp it firmly to the bench with the dish surface uppermost. With the compass set at a radius of 15 cm, step off round the circumference of the disc; this will give you six marks. If you now draw a line from every alternate mark to the centre of the circle, you will have divided the disc into three equal segments. Using a brace and bit, and a drill or spoon-cutting bit of a slightly smaller diameter than the legs, you are ready to drill the leg holes.

It is at this stage that you will have to take extra care. At a point about 8 cm along the three radius lines, drill holes that angle out towards the edges of the disc, this is no easy task as the angle at which the drill enters the wood has to be judged by eye. The legs should be a push fit, no tighter, and they should be tapered slightly so that they go just through the thickness of the seat, but no further.

When you are sure that the legs are a good fit, take them out and cut a wedge out of the 5 cm length that goes through the seat. The legs should now be pushed home, and glued wedges tapped in from above. The wedge should expand the leg across the grain of the seat. In this way it can be banged firmly home without the risk of the seat splitting. When the glue is dry the stubs of the legs that stick through the seat can be cut off and the leg ends cut so that they stand square to the floor.

To retain the character and simplicity of the stool, the wood is given either a good glossy polish or a wax finish.

138 (A) By drawing diagonals find the centre of your slab of wood. (B) Buy or turn three legs which are about 30 cm in length. (C) With a large bow or coping saw cut out the circular seat. (D) With a traditional draw knife, or a rasp, take off the edges so that they are round in section.

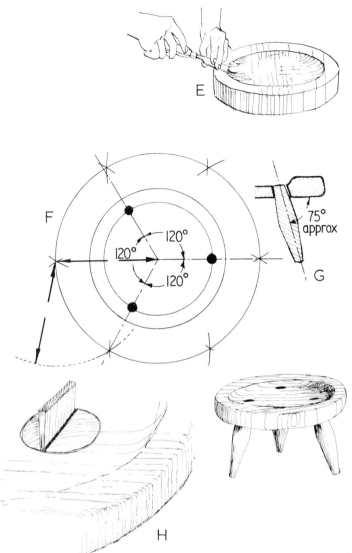

139 (E) Using a gouge make a depression for the seat. (F) Using a compass set at the radius measurement, mark out the position for the legs. (G) The leg holes are drilled at an approximate angle of 75° and angled towards the centre of the seat. (H) Once the slotted legs have been banged into the underneath of the seat, glued wedges are tapped in from above.

140 Nineteenth century turned wooden kitchen ware, bowls and spoons – commonplace articles in a poor man's home (*Rutland County Museum*).

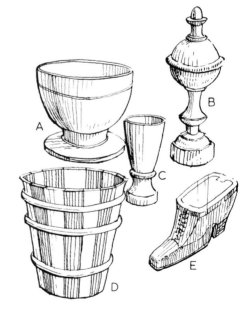

141 (A) A wassail bowl made from the wood lignum vitae. (B) Seventeenth century spice jar, walnut. (C) A spill vase. (D) A cooper made and turned cup. (E) A shoe-shaped snuff box with sliding lid.

142 A commercially-made turned-wood, sewing thread holder, nineteenth century (*Rutland County Museum*).

Treen

Treen is a Saxon word which means 'of the trees' or 'from the trees'. As we have seen, it is now used collectively to describe all the small articles which have been made by the wood turner and carver. Many of these items were for use in the kitchen or dairy, while others were small personal bedroom and wardrobe bits and bobs. Treen is by modern definition that which is small enough to be picked up in one hand, so it can be used to describe something as delicate as a snuff box, or as robust as say a small stool. This definition is loose and is used to describe thousands of objects which are linked only by the fact that they are all made from wood. Another point about treen is that most of the articles have either been replaced by similar ones which are now made of different materials such as metal or plastic, or they are now no longer being used because of some change in fashion or ways of life. Examples of treen which have been replaced by plastics or pottery are such everyday objects as egg-cups, soup bowls, salt pots, napkin rings and rulers – the list is almost endless. Examples of treen which have gone out of common usage are such things as inkpots, seals, braidlooms, bobbin winders, patch boxes, wig stands and corset bones: most of us no longer wear wigs and women no longer sit at home braiding or making lace. For ease of definition I am going to organise treen into three groups – objects made on a lathe; objects made professionally with saws and gouges; and objects made by amateurs as expressions of love.

LATHE-MADE TREEN
This heading covers lathe-made round objects which have been turned from one lump of wood, eg bobbins and egg-cups, objects which have been built up and then turned on the lathe, eg cooper-made bowls, and objects which have been turned on the lathe and then heavily carved, eg candle sticks, butter markers and toys.

The pole and bow lathe were increasingly used from the fifteenth century to make all the objects considered a necessity in the average household. Unseasoned wood was

143 A turned nineteenth century mouse trap. Many ingenious devices were made in wood to catch the ever present pest – when the see-saw action of the cheese tray tripped the stick, the weight fell and squashed the mouse (*Rutland County Museum*).

(*opposite*)
144 Many large households kept a small post box in the hall; this one is interesting in that it is octagonal and has a small drawer for the stamps (*Rutland County Museum*).

120

taken straight from the tree and worked on by the turner. This craft gradually developed into an organised trade with a charter and a guild. The craft flourished well into the nineteenth century, so there are many good examples in museums and antique shops. Some of the most delightful examples of the solid turned ware are the egg-cups and bowls which were so common only a few years ago. Because of the size, the wood turner was able to work in exotic woods such as lignum vitae and ebony, and it is these which are of special interest.

Turners of the seventeenth century enlarged the scope of the craft by glueing up different-coloured woods and using cooper-made bowls and containers. These were put on the lathe and worked so that there was a concentration on the patterns that could be created with the different-coloured woods. The majority of this ware is in the form of bowls, urns, mugs and toys.

Objects which have been turned and then carved are usually the work of two people. The turner would make only the basic shape, which was then handed over to either professional or casual carvers. The majority of this ware was made for the kitchen or dairy – such utensils as butter markers and pastry tools needed to be in the round, but also to have a carved design on their surface. Toys were also often turned and carved; dolls and nursery animals are common examples.

PROFESSIONALLY CARVED TREEN

This group includes mainly objects that were required for every-day usage and which were cut and shaped out of solid lumps of wood. There are many examples to be found and they were for all walks of life, from the primitive spoons and ladles used in poor cottages to ornate snuff boxes for the wealthy. Many of these objects are bewildering – we now find it difficult, and sometimes impossible, to discover their original purpose. There are curious stringed and levered boxes which turn out to be mouse traps, enormous 'cricket bats' which turn out to be washing-beaters. Some of the more curious were used in animal care and husbandry, and we can now only hazard a guess

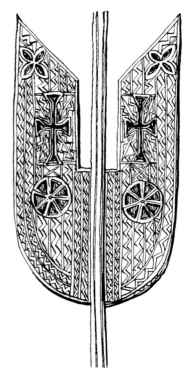

145 A peasant-made, chip-carved distaff from Sibiiu, Romania. The carved motifs on household objects of this type often have religious significance.

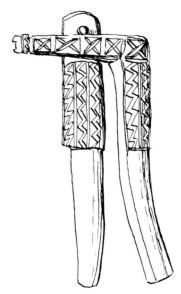

146 A pair of peasant-made, chip-carved nut crackers from Transylvania, carved in the hard and close-grained yew.

122

at just what was done with them. The charm
of many of these items is that they are evoca-
tive and unique examples of an aspect of the
carver's craft that has just faded away.

LOVE TOKENS

Most of the carved items in this group were
made by amateurs in their own homes just
for the pleasure of working with wood. By
definition love tokens were 'one off' items –
often simple chip-carved pieces that were
worked on in the long winter evenings and
later given to a sweetheart. Examples of this
type of carving can be found all over Europe
and America. The tools used were knives
and scrapers and the woods were usually
those commonly found in such areas –
cedar, pine and occasionally exotic woods
such as ebony and mahogany, perhaps
obtained as off-cuts from cabinet and furniture makers.

   Love tokens, whether given in Tudor
times or the middle of the nineteenth
century, usually carried the same patterns.
Twined hearts and joined initials were the
commonest motifs, but some of the Welsh
carvers and American carvers went so far as
to carve very complex 'linked' tokens out of
the one piece of wood. For example linked
spoons, caged birds, carved knots – they
were all intended as symbols of 'together-
ness' and meant to represent the carver who
was bound, tied or captured in love. Many of
the early items, such as the carved corset
rod, were given by the lover to his loved, the
significance being that she wore it secretly
under her clothes and next to her heart.

Letter-Knife Love Token

For this project you will need a piece of
green wood – straight from the tree. This
will not only give you a broader understanding of your material, but it will also give you
an excuse for a walk in the country. You are
looking for a piece of wood that is about 30
cm long and about 5 cm thick; the wood
species is important – I think a piece of blackthorn root would be ideal. When you have
found your piece of wood, and it would be
more interesting if it were knotted and had a
shape which in itself was suggestive, then

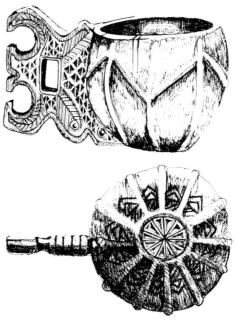

147   Side and bottom view of a wooden cup,
Romania. Peasant-made, chip-carved objects of
this type are to be considered in the same class as
Welsh loving spoons, as they were given as tokens
of love.

123

148 Butter markers and pastry rollers (lime?). Although considered as very ordinary objects, the carving on many butter markers is of a very high standard (*Rutland County Museum*).

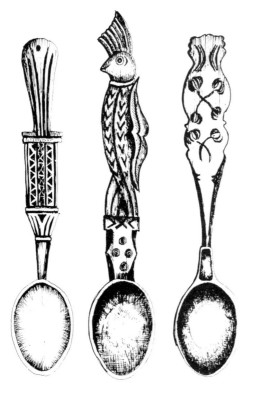

149 Love token spoons, Transylvania. The chip-carved designs are similar to those found on earthenware pottery of Central Europe and Pioneer American wood carving.

150 Chip-carved busks or corset rods, eighteenth century. Obviously carved by a lover, they are beautiful to look at, but one wonders if they were ever really worn.

151 A beautiful carved spoon and fork with forget-me-not design (*Rutland County Museum*).

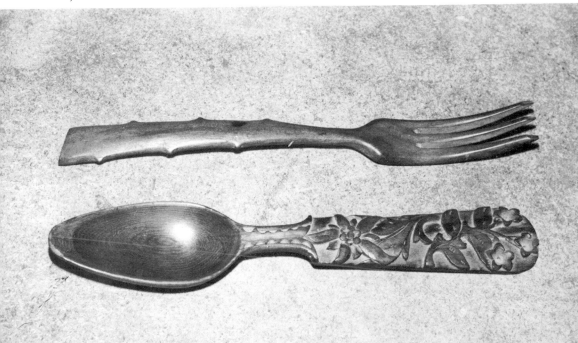

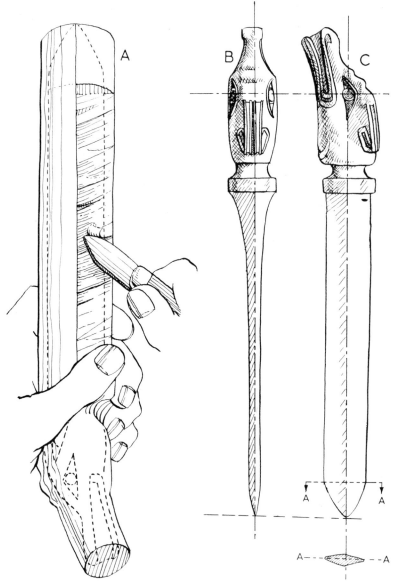

152 (A) Using a penknife the blade of the wooden paper knife is cut to shape, always cut away from your body. (B) Top view of the knife. (C) Side view.

you can start to carve. The only equipment you will need is a good sharp clasp knife, and several grades of sandpaper.

The size and shape of your material will dictate the precise design, but measure the width of your hand on one end of the wood, and then make a mark. Hold the piece of wood by the end that will eventually be the handle, and carve the other end so that it is flat in section and blade-shaped. The blade section of the carving should be as broad and flat as the wood will allow, and the handle

153 A gentleman's portable egg cup. In this photograph the top is in place, but it can be removed and inside there is another foot for the top half of the cup – so there are in fact two egg cups (*Permission Mrs J. Duncan*).

should be round in section and shaped into whatever beast, pattern or motif the shape of the wood suggests. The piece of wood that I have illustrated seemed to suggest a dog's head, so I used that as the basis for my carving. If the wood is the hard, knarled, twisted variety that is often found at the root end of a piece of blackthorn, then you might be lucky and find a piece which is large enough to make a walking stick. With this type of free carving or whittling, it is important that you look for naturally occurring shapes and twists in the wood and then use them to advantage. If you live by the sea shore then drift wood is just perfect for whittling; more often than not it already has a shape which is beautiful, and sometimes the wood is exotic, old and very well seasoned.

When you have shaped the wood to your satisfaction it will need to be 'finished'. For this I use graded sandpapers and rub in the direction of the grain. Use the sandpapers with caution, or the surface of the wood will be damaged – stroke rather than scour, and never use a sandpaper block across the grain.

When the wood is completely dry, use a smooth cloth and work in some oil; ethnic carvers use animal grease and butter fats, but a drop of linseed oil is as good as anything. Use as much oil as the wood will take and when it is dry give it a liberal coating of furniture wax. A carved object of this character will improve in patina and shape with use and handling.

6

INLAY, MARQUETRY AND TUNBRIDGE WARE

Inlay, marquetry and Tunbridging are all similar methods of fixing decorative woods onto, or into the surface of more common woods.

The processes, which use slightly different techniques, all have a history which goes back as far as the Egyptians and the Greeks. Many of the early Egyptian Third Dynasty boxes and coffins were made of several layers of decorative woods. Although these techniques can be a process of concealment to cover up poor work, this isn't usually the case.

Inlay

Although there are many examples of ethnic inlaying techniques which use such exotic materials as mother of pearl and ivory, we, for simplification, will concentrate on what we could loosely describe as modern European and English furniture inlay. Inlaying is the name given to a method of building up a decorative or patterned surface from various coloured woods. Inlaying and marquetry are similar; the main difference is that inlaying refers to the 'laying in' of little blocks of wood, where as marquetry refers

(*left*)
154   Egyptian ebony and ivory inlaid cosmetics casket. Nearly all the wood working techniques that we know today were understood by the Egyptian carpenters 5000 years ago. During this period the carvers were working with very sophisticated wood laminates and veneers.

(*below*)
155   A wooden fish inlaid with mother-of-pearl, Eastern Solomon Islands. Although there are many examples of Oceanic chip carving where the cut-away areas are filled with stiff white mastic, inlay work is peculiar to the Solomon Islands area. Most of the pattern and designs on this work are considered functional, with active magical significance.

156 Wood and ivory inlay, Portuguese, thought to be late eighteenth century. The ebony inlay is secured to the light oak ground by small ivory pins, which relate to the overall design theme.

157 An inlaid 'Nonesuch' chest. The design is supposed to represent Henry VIII's Surrey pleasure palace of Nonesuch, which was pulled down, it is thought, in the eighteenth century. Known as intarsia, this type of repeated inlay banding became a common feature on cheap mass-produced boxes of later periods. The inlay was made up in lengths, and then cut off as required. The chest is of dark oak, with bog oak and cherry inlay.

to the sticking on of fine sheets of wood.

As a method of decorating boxes and chests, inlaying became enormously popular in the fourteenth and fifteenth centuries. On some of the very early Venetian and Italian work the craftsmen used a combination of materials. Some of the most characteristic work of this period uses such wide ranging inlays as tortoise shell, mother of pearl, ivory and brass. Inlaying of coloured woods developed alongside the great technological achievements of the sixteenth and seventeenth centuries. Mechanised saw mills, and thin saw blades made it possible to control the cutting of wood to such a fine degree that it was economically viable to use inlay or intarsia to a greater extent. Unlike marquetry, inlaying is primarily a wood carver's craft in that it is first of all necessary to carve out a ground pattern into which the coloured mosaic can be bedded. In the early European inlay work the designs tended to be geometrical, and the box and chest makers concentrated on patterns and motifs which gained much of their effect by using optical and perspective illusions. Many of the pieces made in the seventeenth century used exotic woods which were imported from such places as the East Indies and the Americas, and as the technique became more fashionable it became more excessive and florid. By the end of the eighteenth century the designs on the chests and boxes were characterized by masses of flowers and vivid colour. The actual technique of laying in the woods calls for precision, patience, an attention to detail, and considerable knowledge of wood types.

METHOD

The design must first of all be worked out on paper and fully considered and it might be better if first attempts were restricted to simple geometrical shapes. Traditionally the initial design was pricked out through the sheet of paper which was then dusted with coloured powder. The powder was pushed through this first sheet onto other papers, and so the carver had several copies of the master design. This rather messy method is now no longer strictly necessary, it is easier to trace the original design. Once the various elements of the pattern have been drawn out on paper they can be cut out and stuck to pieces of wood of the right thickness and colour. A suitable thickness for inlay is about 1 cm, but this is relative to the materials that you have at hand.

The total design is now drawn out on a base board, and then with a gouge and chisel, it can be cut out and recessed to a depth of just under 1 cm. The individual pieces of the design can be cut out with a fine saw. Once all the separate elements of the design have been cut, they can be placed into the pattern recess in the base board, – if you have been careful with the cutting they should be a tight fit. Once you are pleased with the effect, remove the inlay pieces, glue the recess with a clean, lump-free P.V.A. glue, and then replace the inlay. When you

158 Bohemian cabinet, seventeenth century. The design of this cabinet is obviously heavily influenced by German and Russian work of the same period. The inlay techniques and the counterchanging of patterns are similar to those used by the French 'Boulle' workers of the early eighteenth century.

are sure all the pieces fit, tap them home firmly with a hammer.

When the work is dry, the proud surface of the design can be sanded down to the level of the base board, and then polished and waxed.

INLAY DESIGN ON EXISTING FURNITURE

For this project you will need a box, chest, chair back, etc, on which you want the design to be placed. Note the wood on which you are going to work must be at least 3 cm thick. This whole design project is based on a simple repeated 3 cm square motif, – so you must obtain a chisel of that width, or slightly revise the measurements.

Mark out the border on the piece of furniture. This must measure 3 cm, and be

159 The layout for this project is very simple, but the measurements must be 'tight' and precise. (A) This banding is set in from the edge of the worked surface by a 1cm margin – this is critical, and considerable care will have to be taken with the top edge where the grain is short. (B) Apart from obvious colour variations, the only other pattern factor is the arrangement of the direction of the grain on the inlay blocks. Note – the inlay blocks must never be placed end-grain uppermost. When the blocks are set in the channel, it is important that they are slightly 'proud', then they can be sanded flush with the main surface.

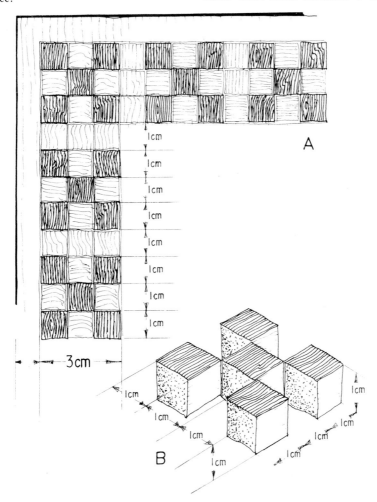

A

B

3cm

131

recessed to a depth of just under 1 cm. In no instance should the depth of the rebate exceed 1 cm.

As you can see from the illustration, the motif is based on a square of 3 cm which contains five small dark squares and four small light squares. This motif, which I shall refer to as a 'five square' motif, is separated from its neighbouring 'five square' motif by a space of 1 cm.

If you give a quick count you will see that you need slightly more light squares than dark. Before marking out the border you must calculate the squares so that the border turns on a 'five square' motif at the corners. The main section of the groove can be cut with a plough, but at the corners you will have to use a chisel to clean up the angles.

Once you have chosen two suitable woods for the inlay, mark them out and cut them up into small cubes measuring 1 cm × 1 cm × 1 cm. Part of the charm of inlay is in the slight irregularities that occur in the design, but nevertheless it is vital that all cuts are as accurate as possible.

Once the cubes are ready, it is time to have a 'dry run' and lay out the design as illustrated. If, when you get to the turning point of the groove you find that your cutting is slightly at fault, rather than cut a few squares smaller, it is better to make an adjustment on several groups. In this way the slight change in size will be less noticeable. Glueing is relatively straightforward, as long as the groove is well organised, and not too deep. Use clean, fresh, lump-free P.V.A. glue. Be generous, but don't splash it about as it does stain certain woods. Once all the cubes are in place and a tight fit, they can be hammered home. When the work is dry the surface can be sanded until the blocks are at the same level as the base wood. Finally the total surface can be waxed and polished.

NB: The grain of the inlay blocks can run with or across the grain of the base wood, but there should be no visible end grain.

Marquetry

Marquetry is the name given to the process of cutting fine sheets of wood, all of an equal thickness, and bedding them in glue on a

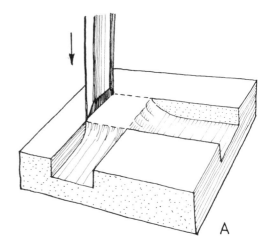

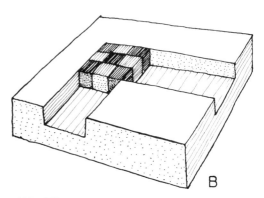

160 When the channels have been cut with the plough plane, or scratch stock, the corners have to be cut and cleaned up with a flat chisel. Care must be taken that areas of short-grain are not broken away. (B) The inlaid blocks should be a tight fit, and then tapped home with a hammer. There should be plenty of glue in the groove; this will help to fill out any poor joints.

(above)

161 Detail of a floral motif from a cabinet, late seventeenth century, English. The furniture makers of this period were using woods, tortoise shell and mother-of-pearl in a beautiful naturalistic floral style which was influenced by the marquetry workers of France and Holland.

(left)

162 A characteristic 'Boulle' design motif, late seventeenth century, French. Andre Charles Boulle had a studio workshop in the Louvre and made furniture exclusively for King Louis XIV. A feature of Boulle work is the technique of placing together two thin sheets of say metal and tortoise shell, cutting a design through both sheets, and then counter-changing the pieces. This method of marquetry called for considerable design care, but at the same time it was very economical in its use of materials.

163 A rosewood veneered secretaire, by Rodger La Croix, middle of the eighteenth century. The design of this piece of furniture is so organised that the herring-bone pattern on the doors conceals the vertical breaks.

base board. It is thought that marquetry is perhaps the final stage in the development of inlay. As the exotic and rare woods were difficult and expensive to obtain, so the craftsmen, for reasons of economy, looked for ways of cutting the inlay pieces thinner. Followed to its logical conclusion, this would naturally result in marquetry. Traditionally in this process the woods are tinted, scorched, or coloured, arranged, and let into a veneered surface. There is no need for the base wood to be recessed and carved, as in inlay.

During the fifteenth century in England and Europe, marquetry expressed itself in elaborate 'architectural' and perspective panels on boxes, cupboards and chests. By the sixteenth and seventeenth centuries furniture marquetry had evolved into a style which was distinctive for its flowing lines, and the profusion of bright flowers, animals, ribbons and swags. The development of marquetry reached a peak in France in the seventeenth century, when Pierre and André Boulle created designs which used brass and ebony. Examples of English work

164 Cabinet by Boulle, French, seventeenth century. The upper parts of this cabinet are inlaid with purple wood, tortoise shell, pewter, brass and ebony. The floral motifs are characteristic of the period, and are considered to be really fine examples of the Boulle marquetry technique.

of this period, and of the eighteenth and nineteenth centuries, tended to be restrained and subtle in line and colour. This was not the case with continental work which delighted in sumptuous colours, full-bodied patterns, exaggerated and extraordinary displays of skill and expertise. Modern marquetry by comparison is dull and rather feeble in design, but really good examples can still be found on 'art' and exhibition pieces. Although marquetry isn't now used commonly on furniture it is still a valid medium for design and colour expression, and there is no doubt in my mind that a working knowledge of marquetry techniques provides a valuable addition to wood carving skills.

METHOD
Veneers are now best obtained in sanded, thin, cut sheets which are ready to use. Marquetry is a craft which can either be large, bold, and inspired by dramatic ethnic pattern, or it can be 'quiet', small, and a means of traditional pictorial expression.

In the past, marquetry designs were first of all worked out on paper, and then the lines of the pattern pricked through at regular intervals. Through the holes of this master design asphatum powder was dusted onto secondary pieces of paper – when these were heated, they became perfect copies of the original. These pattern copies were then cut and stuck to veneers of the appropriate grain and colour. The marqueteurs of the past often needed to cut dozens of pieces the same pattern, so they made a sandwich of the various marquetry sheets and cut them on a saw, seat and clamp apparatus, known as a marquetry cutter's 'donkey'. As we are primarily interested only in 'one-offs' rather than mass production, I would suggest that working with a craft knife would be the best cutting method, and the use of tracing paper the simplest method of pattern transference. Unlike veneering, marquetry is a technique of cutting, glueing and pressing, and because the pieces of the design are small and delicate, the use of water, and hot hammering, (as in veneering) is not necessary or suitable. The various elements of the design are drawn out onto separate pieces of paper, and then stuck to the selected veneers. As marquetry is basically a process of fitting together lots of small pieces of wood, rather like a jigsaw puzzle, it is vital that the individual pieces are cut out with care and precision.

For simple designs, when several pieces have been cut, they can be used as edge guides for subsequent elements. If, on the other hand, your design is complex and contains many small parts, then there is another knife cutting method which is perhaps more suitable. First of all, draw out the design on the veneer that is going to form the 'ground'. If, for example, the design consists of a cottage in a meadow, then the bulk of the 'ground' will be the meadow. Choose a suitable veneer which is at least as large as the picture and draw out the design. Starting with the largest design element, say the roof of the cottage, cut round and through on the base veneer. You should now have a piece of veneer onto which is drawn the design, and in which there is a roof-shaped hole. This hole can be moved around over a suitable veneer until you find a grain and colour that is just right. The decorative veneer can then be cut, and with sticky tape fixed into the roof-shaped hole in the base veneer. Continue in this fashion until all the design elements on the base wood have been replaced with decorative veneers. You should finish up with a complete design with pieces of sticky tape all over its back. Now, with great care, stick tape to the front of the design and remove the tape from the back. You will now require a base board of 'half inch' ply which is slightly bigger than your design, also a piece of cheap veneer which can be mounted on the back. This compensates for any twisting or tension that takes place.

Freshly made P.V.A. glue is now applied to the back of the board, and the piece of compensating veneer placed in position. The board is now turned over, given a coat of glue, and the marquetry design put into place. It can then be covered with newspaper and placed in a press. After a couple of days, the work can be taken out of the press and the tape and newspaper removed. Finally, the work must be cleaned up with fine glass paper, polished and waxed.

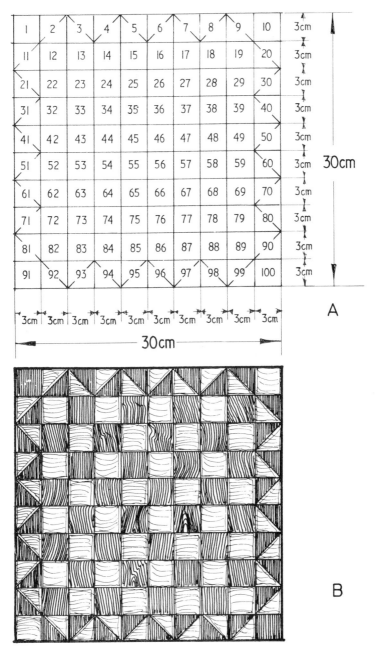

A

B

165 (A) The grid for this chess board is based on 100 squares, which are numbered for simple and direct reference. You will need a base board of ½″ ply which measures 30 cm × 30 cm, and this must be marked out into 3 cm squares. (B) The design is organised so that there is an equal interchange between dark and light woods. I have also made the direction of the grain a feature, but this isn't critical.

137

A MARQUETRY CHESS BOARD,
AND DESIGNS FOR CHESSMEN

For this project you will need a piece of half inch ply 30 cm × 30 cm, one sheet of the cheapest compensating veneer for the back of the ply, 450 sq cm of a dark marquetry veneer, and 450 sq cm of a light veneer. The choice of the veneer depends on your personal preference, and commercial availability, but I suggest that you ask for an 'odd ends bundle'. At the end of this section, there is a short list of veneers which at this moment in time are easily obtainable in England.

Mark out the ply base board diagonally, quarter the sides, and then with care mark out the board into squares of 3 cm, and number them as illustrated. (The numbers are for easy reference). This marquetry project is especially suitable for beginners because they will be required to measure and cut precisely, no easy task. If you refer to the illustration, you will see that you are going to need, 34 dark squares, 34 light squares, 32 dark triangles, and 32 light triangles. For the cutting of the veneer you will need a good sharp craft knife, a set square, and a metal straight edge. The rest is up to you. Lay out the pieces as illustrated and tape them together. When all the pieces are taped, prepare the board with a suitable glue, place the marquetry in position, and put in a clamp or press.

When the glue is dry the marquetry can be sanded, polished and waxed.

Chessmen
The chessmen are basically an exercise in turning and whittling but as it will be constantly necessary to refer to the chess board for colour and proportion data, I have included them in this section.

There are two ways of approaching this task: you can either buy ready-turned 1″ pole, and hand-carve all the grooves, or you can do all the ground work on a lathe.

As you can see from the illustrations, the simplest way of turning the individual pieces is to use the maximum width of the lathe, turn the grooves, and then cut up the pole when the individual pieces have been realised.

Finishing
King The head of the king suggests a high 'roof' section. This is best achieved with a small hand knife.

Queen The head of the queen is almost identical with that of the king, the only difference being scale and the fact that the angle of the 'roof' springs straight out of the shoulder. There is no neck.

Castle The top of the castle, is a straightforward cross castellation, a flat cross in section.

Bishop The bishop has traditional characteristics. The slot is best cut out with a fine saw and chisel.

Knight The head of the knight is cylindrical. The helmet is relief-carved, and then punch-textured.

Pawn The pawn is the most difficult piece to make as its head is round. This calls for careful lathe work, and a finish with a knife and fine sand paper.

MARQUETRY VENEERS LIST
Ash English
A light-coloured wood with strong brown heart section, often with interesting mottle figure.

Birch Canadian
A well-figured wood which can be obtained in white or dark.

Ebony
An expensive dark brown/black wood which can only be obtained in narrow widths, up to about 7″.

Mahogany
There are many varieties, all with very individual characteristics, dapple figure, bees wing, fiddle back, etc. The colours tend to range from red/brown, to yellow/orange.

Maple, Birds Eye
Available in big sheets with good figuring. Lays better when thick gauge.

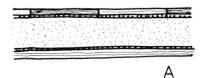

A

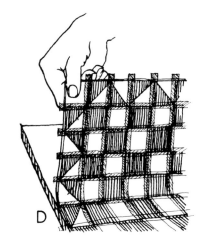

D

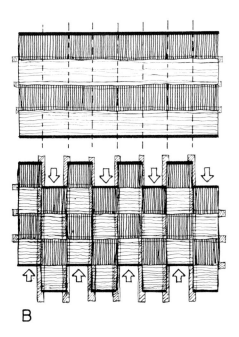

B

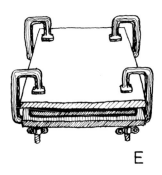

E

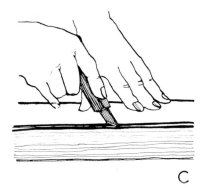

C

166 (A) A cross section which shows the marquetry veneers, the ½″ ply or block board, and
the sheet of cheap compensating veneer.

(B) Ideally for our design you would start off with
eight strips of veneer, but this isn't always possible, especially if you are using 'end bundle'
pieces. When you tape the pieces together, use
masking tape, or brown parcel tape.

(C) When cutting the veneer always use a metal
straight edge. When cutting with the grain be
careful, as some varieties of veneer are liable to
split.

(D) If the pieces of the design are taped together,
setting out the veneer should be relatively
simple. If you use a lump free P.V.A. glue, time
and speed aren't critical, and you will have time
for fine adjustment.

(E) Before you place the work in the press, make
sure all the glued surfaces are covered with newspaper. The press illustrated is made from four G
clamps and stout boards.

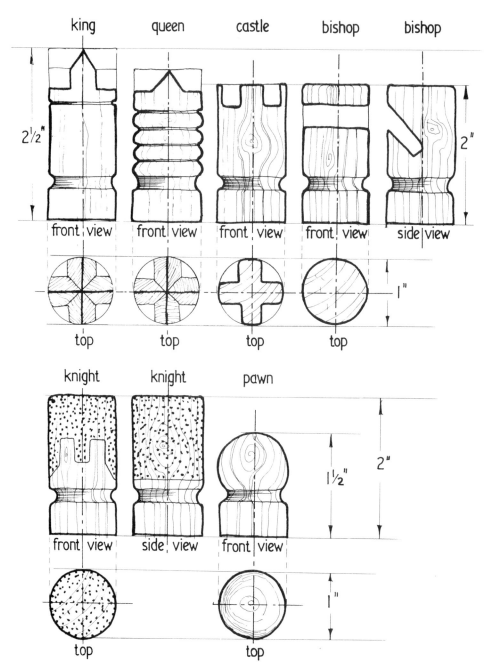

167 The chessmen are based on the simplest turned shapes; carving is minimal. The pieces are all 1″ diameter; this simplifies the turning process, and relates to the measurements of the marquetry chess board.

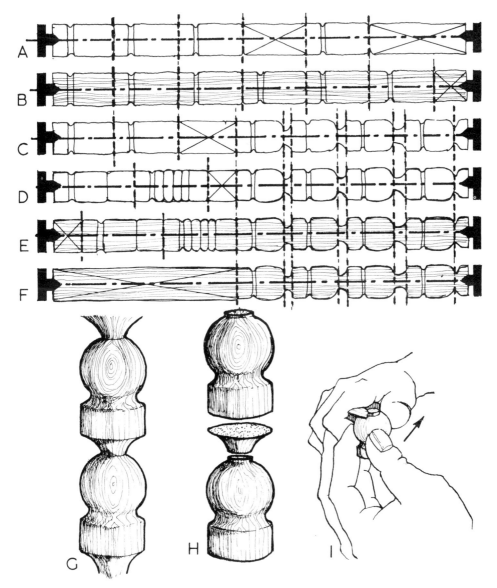

168 This diagrammatical layout illustrates how the chess pieces are related to the width of the lathe. Reading from left to right the pieces are:

(A) bishop, castle, bishop, waste, bishop, waste
(B) bishop, bishop, castle, knight, knight, castle, waste
(C) knight, knight, waste, pawn, pawn, pawn, pawn
(D) king, queen, waste, pawn, pawn, pawn, pawn
(E) waste, king, queen, pawn, pawn, pawn, pawn
(F) spare wood, pawn, pawn, pawn, pawn.

Although I have used two different woods, the pieces could of course be made from the same wood, and then coloured; this must be a matter of personal choice.

(G) Two pawns when they are part of the turned pole.
(H) Cutting sequence for the pawns.
(I) The waste knob on top of the pawn is best cut off with a sharp hand knife and then sanded.

141

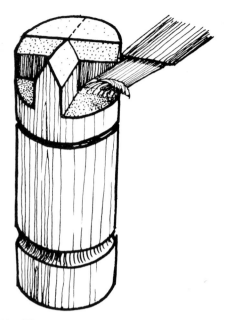

169 The carved heads of the chessmen are best cut with a small hand knife. There is no simple method, so practise with scrap turnings.

Oak, English, Russian, Japanese, Australian

All these woods have good characteristics and are relatively easy to obtain. The English is fine silver-grained with good figures, while the Australian tends to have a large bold figure. Ask to see several varieties.

Padouk, Indian

A beautiful reddish/orange/brown wood which has a very distinctive narrow, striped, figure pattern.

Rosewood

There are several varieties, all of which range in colour from brown to purple. Very pleasant to use.

Sycamore, English

A good hard wood, which can be obtained in white, grey, silver and brown. Some of these colours are obtained by chemical dipping.

Walnut

This wood can be obtained in many varieties, colours, figures and sizes. Pleasant to

use, with many characteristics which make it suitable for large exhibition pieces. Colours range from shades of purple to black/brown.

Tunbridge Ware

Tunbridge ware is a unique inlay technique which was practised in England during the late seventeenth, eighteenth and nineteenth centuries. There are many similarities between Tunbridge ware and early English inlay, but as far as I know, the method and application are completely unconnected.

The wares were made in small rural workshops in Tunbridge Wells, Kent, England, and were considered by the Victorian visitors to the spa town as valid and desirable works of art. In my opinion the ware hasn't any great artistic merit, but viewed as another method of inlay, it is extremely interesting, and has great wood craft possibilities. Traditionally the ware was confined to small boxes, tables, toys, picture frames, games boards, and platters, and limited to such design themes as, flowers, romantic ruins, and simple optical patterns. There is no reason why the technique cannot be broadened and related to modern art/craft design. Indeed, I have seen abstracted, non-functional, sculpture which used a larger version of the technique to great effect. The main possibility of relating the technique to modern carving and wood crafts, is its potential for repeated pattern.

METHOD

Basically, Tunbridging is a method of mass producing mosaic motifs in wood. The design is first of all worked out on paper, and then organised so that the various elements of the design are broken down into coloured squares. Wooden rods are cut so they have the end grain along one edge, then coloured, glued, and tied together so that they look rather like bundles of pencils. It is a section through the bundle that relates to the original 'squared up' design. When the glue is dry, the bundle is placed in a guillotine, (or disc saw), and it is cut up into fine slices. With the traditional Tunbridge ware the designs were organised so that the slices of

142

170　A Victorian Tunbridge ware box – the illustration shows a characteristic romantic scene. The mosaic ware was the final stage in a tradition which covered about three hundred years. Some designs used as many as 150 different coloured woods, all of which had to be cut and glued by hand. The ware represents what has since been described as Victorian 'art ware' at its best.

171 A miniature Tunbridge cabinet which is veneered with the fine cube mosaic, and also the older and more traditional Vandyke pattern marquetry.

mosaic slotted together forming a complete design. It is important that in the design stages the patterns are consciously thought of as interlocking pieces. In the final stages of the technique, the mosaics are mounted up on a base board as in marquetry.

TUNBRIDGE WARE PATTERN FOR A DECORATIVE OR FUNCTIONAL SURFACE
As you can see from the illustration the design motif contains 23 dark squares and 15 light squares. The actual size of the squares isn't critical, but I would suggest something like 5 mm.

Cut or buy two planks of wood, one dark, the other light. Ideal wood types are mahogany, and a knot-free Parana pine. The planks must measure 5 mm thick, 20 cm wide and 100 cm long. It is important that the wood is straight-grained and free from knots.

The two planks must be cut, mechanically if possible, along their entire length, into pieces 5 mm wide. You should now have two piles of wooden rods that measure 5 mm × 5 mm × 20 cm long. These rods must be glued and placed into bundles so

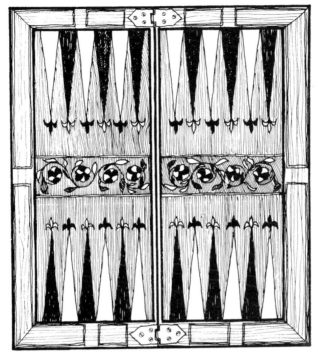

that their end sections correspond to the motif as illustrated. Clamping is rather tricky, but wrapping with newspaper, and then binding with string is perhaps the simplest answer. When the glue is dry, the bundles of rods can be cut across their lengths into 5 mm slices. From direct observation you will see that the thickness of the total mosaic is 5 mm, so it is important that the thickness of the slices is controlled and constant. Traditionally the slices were cut about ⅙″ thick. If the mosaics are to be mounted onto the surface of an existing piece of furniture, then it is relatively straight forward. If, on the other hand, the work is to be mounted onto a fresh base board, then this will have to have a piece of compensating veneer glued to its back.

For a 'dry run', arrange the slices as illustrated, and tape them together so that they form a tight sheet. Prepare the surface onto which they are to go, and glue with a fresh, lump-free, P.V.A. glue. As there is bound to be considerable variation in mosaic thickness it will be necessary to cover the whole surface with several layers of newspaper before pressing. When the work is completely dry, smooth down, polish and wax.

172 Marquetry and inlaid Tunbridge backgammon board. Boards of this type and design were made at Tunbridge in the late seventeenth century, and they represent the early stages in the Tunbridge ware development.

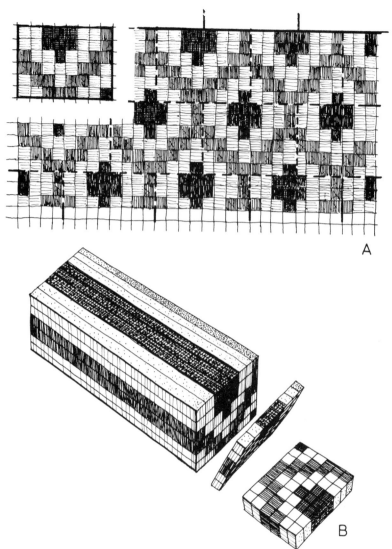

173 (A) The grid for this design is based on a motif which contains 48 coloured wooden sticks. End section slices combine to form a pattern which has its roots in ethnic carpet design.

(B) The section end slices in this instance are cut about 5 mm thick, but traditionally they were cut to a thickness of about 1 mm.

CONCLUSION

Design Appreciation

A process of work, in this case carving, calls for an understanding of tools, techniques, and materials. It is the mark of a true craftsman that he is in sympathy, not only with the immediate fashions and styles of his period, but with ideas of the past. At the same time he must be moving forward in a state of continuous exploration and experimentation. The methods, tools and techniques play a major part in the formation of any craft, but the materials must always be fully considered and approached with feeling, and not with aggressive domination. There are, within the concept of design, certain characteristics which can be recognised as belonging to say, pottery, weaving, or carving. The materials used will always retain their character and struggle against unsuitable forms. The nature and design of any single piece of carving is rarely accidental, as they relate to the materials, the shape of the tools, and the state of mind of the carver.

The roots of most practical design gain strength from a willingness to use the tools with awareness and also a desire to work within the limitations of the materials. Design is to a great extent a matter of common sense and intelligent application of self. I would say that a carver's skill is the result of effort and an urge to create. Having said this, all craftsmen will flourish if they are keen and retain a forward-looking enthusiasm based on sound practical knowledge.

A student of wood carving must also be a student of design, he must not only be able to use his hands, but he must keep his eyes and mind open. It is correct that a student carver's first attempts should relate to great works of the past, but there will come a point when he has to carve in a manner which is unique to himself.

I think it fair to say that in the past craftsmen were forced by limited communications to work within the small confines of their immediate cultural environment. We are now in a period which is historically unique in that increased media and travel communications have produced a situation where craft influences tend to be global rather than tribal. No longer are we restricted to our relatively provincial craft traditions, we are able to look outside the society in which we live, and draw on unfamiliar cultures for design inspiration. World travel, television and literature have rekindled in most artist/craftsmen an awareness of the innocence and naivety of ethnic design. The craft of wood carving is especially significant in this climate of discovery as, in most cultures, carving is an important part of a long tradition.

Primitive carvers, because of their isolation, work in an atmosphere which is free from 'soul-searching'. Ethnic carvers don't want to know why they carve certain forms, patterns and designs; they are more concerned with the function of the carving. We who live in industrial societies are no longer primarily concerned with the functional aspects of wood carving, we are generally more involved with craft elements which relate to aesthetic design. This remoteness from wood carving as a functional craft is perhaps the essence of our struggle. The medieval misericord carvers knew what was expected of them, African mask carvers understand that they are revealing the spirit

147

that hides within the wood, Victorian treen carvers understood that bowls had to fit the hand and be water resistant: these carvers were faced only with problems of function. For us to get to grips with good considered design, we must become involved with aesthetics. The dictionary describes aesthetics as, 'the theory or philosophy of the perception of the beautiful'. No longer are we carvers who are required to make simple, easily understood, functional, forms; we are now artist-carvers whose main aim is to make objects that please the eye.

In the past, design sprang from natural forms, and it is still generally true that natural form is the carver's foremost inspirational criterion. The danger that confronts a student carver is that of allowing preconceived ideas to dominate his design thinking. A carver who is true to himself must translate and draw inspiration from the work of other societies and historical periods, but he at the same time must create work that is 'direct' and related to his own environmental and cultural experience.

Texture

When in wood carving we refer to texture, we are not talking about superficial finish that is applied when the carving is complete. By texture we mean a wood surface that is the natural result of sympathetic use of the carver's tools. Many students new to carving seek to 'finish' their work, and this usually takes the form of heavy sandpapering. All they in fact succeed in doing is removing the marks and character of their original efforts. Wood has a structure and grain that must be 'brought out', and this can only be achieved by skilful and delicate use of the correct tools. If the surface of the wood is attacked with the wrong tools and heavy hands, the carving becomes emasculated, and might as well be made from plastic.

Texture depends on the carver fully understanding what it is he is carving, all the cuts and marks of the tools must be positive. Bold curves must be emphasised, smooth convex surfaces must be clean and uncomplicated. Bad carving is usually marked by confusion of line, and the scratchy use of blunt tools. With carving, the very marks left by the tools are evidence of whether or not those tools have been used correctly. In England during the nineteenth century the carvers were so obsessed with outward finish that they became totally dependent on smooth, machined surfaces. Ethnic carvers might perhaps leave large areas of their carving in a direct adzed state, and then polish other areas to a smooth almost glazed shine: it is this use of considered texture that we must try to develop.

Many different textures could be described as a final finish: a broad gouge leaves a characteristic mark and a scoop adze leaves another, but each in its own way is a perfect finish. In most cases the finish and texture of the wood will not just happen, they must be encouraged and consciously organised. Over-working of a surface is also a danger, a carving that is fussy and minutely worked often only succeeds in loosing all vitality and credibility.

The tools can be used efficiently only in a certain way and direction, and it is this flow of tool marks that helps our eyes and our minds to appreciate the final form. A carved surface which has been 'stressed' or broken with a machine tool, certainly has texture, but it is doubtful whether this artificial marking does anything for the final carving. Good and purposeful tool marks should encourage our eyes to move over and around the carved form. It must be remembered that the depth and quality of the individual cuts can be used to emphasise the lightness and tonal characteristics of the carving. Textural finish can be appropriate if it helps to describe the carved form. All marks must be purposeful and positive.

Form

The term 'form', so far as the carver is concerned, is a way of describing the actual shape and character of the carving.

Forms in nature are the direct result of internal and external pressures and influences which come to bear upon the growing structures. With carving, it is the carver himself who is responsible for making decisions which form his work, which is why the carver must be aware of the factors which make one particular form or shape better than another. Within nature, that which we consider to be beautiful is always organised on pure logic, mathematical stresses, and mechanical laws. Shells, leaf cells, crystals, etc, etc, are all the result of growth, function, and the rightness of materials.

The carver often has to compete with nature as he is constructing shapes and forms which endeavour to use the available material in the most efficient way. If the carver is sensitive, and appreciates the subtle characteristics of his tools and materials, he will not need to struggle to oppose and compete with nature. If he is true to his craft, natural forms will be the only logical answer to his design problems.

Drawing

As a budding carver, it would be a great advantage to have a knowledge and understanding of drawing. Most carvers of the past needed to be able to put their ideas and imaginings down on paper. If the carver is going to work on a particular form, it is vital that he becomes as familiar with the projections of his 'mind's eye' as possible. Drawing is one of the ways that the craftsman organises his mind, his plans and makes exact predictions of shape and form. Drawing is a matter of illusion and symbolization.

Having said all this, we come down to the basics. How is it done? You will need a good soft pencil, plenty of stiff white paper (matt), and a sketch book. As a carver you will be primarily concerned with expressions of mass and form, and not effect, you will be drawing for your own reference rather than for exhibition. When you want to draw a sphere, it will first of all appear on the flat paper as a circle. By shading one half of the circle you create the illusion of a three-dimensional, solid form. For most drawing it is sufficient to create the illusion by the use of line, but this illusion can be strengthened by the use of tone or shadow. You must always assume that your subjects are so placed that they are in strong light on one side and in shadow on the other. If you place

an egg on a matt surface near a window, you will see that the tones on the surface of the egg gradually get darker on the side of the egg that is furthest away from the window. When you draw this egg, it is only by the use of shading or tone that the shape of the egg is fully realised. You will also notice that the shading or tone variations are so subtle that they appear to have no beginning or end. One of your first exercises must be the drawing of tones on such simple shapes as tubes, balls, cubes, etc. For the carver, drawing is a means to an end, not the end in itself, so once you have discovered that three-dimensional illusion on a flat surface is created by the use of tone, then the rest is just practice, practice, and then more practice.

There are instances, when drawing say a concave dish shape, or a hole in a flat surface, where, because of the position of the tone, it is difficult for our eyes and minds to decide whether the drawn shape is concave, or convex. Then drawn lines describing the surface planes have to be used. Let us say that you have drawn a dish shape which has been cut in a flat slab of wood and you have applied tone to the side of the dish that is in shadow. If the eye is still confused, then you must draw lines which describe the form more fully. One of the best ways of doing this is to imagine that a snail has crawled slowly across the surface of the wood, down into the depression and then up the other side. If you also imagine that the snail has in its moving drawn a line on the surface of the wood, then you will also be able to see that the line left by the snail fully describes the form. If, when you are drawing, you let your pencil move over an imaginary form, then the drawing will begin to suggest more fully form, space, light and mass.

Once you have made progress with your struggle to draw, then it is time to get on with the carving.

Finally, if in your carving you can let the cutting tools describe and move across the surface of the wood, much as your pencil moved across imaginary shapes you will be well on the way to a fuller realisation of form and textural subtlety.

GLOSSARY OF TOOLS

Adze The adze was one of the earliest tools known to man. Made of bone, bronze, stone and iron the adze is the main wood cutting tool of primitive people. In use it is swung like a pendulum, and the heavy cutting edge removes scoops of wood.

Auger This early type of drill or hole-borer was still used by English and European wheel-wrights well into the nineteenth century. Looking rather like a spoon mounted in a wooden handle, it was hand-turned, and the cutting edge removed thin discs of wood.

Awl The awl looked like an auger but it was primarily used for piercing holes.

Axe The axe has more or less the same characteristics as the adze, the main difference being that the axe was used for the initial wood preparation, rather than the shaping.

Bench Used since Roman times the bench has existed in many forms. A 'horse' or trestle which had four peg legs was the earliest type. It gradually developed until it looked like a large table with a thick plank top, which usually had rows of holes with bench stops or primitive holdfasts.

Bench Stop A wedge or peg of wood which sticks up through the surface of the bench and stops the wood that is being worked from sliding forward.

Bevel This essential tool comes in all shapes and designs, but basically it is two flat strips of wood or metal with a pivot in the middle. The arms of the bevel can be adjusted so that the angle at which they cross can be fixed. A bevel is used to draw angles of a set and predetermined size.

Bow Drill This rather complicated tool was used by ancient Egyptian wood workers, and it remained in use in various parts of the world right up until the nineteenth century. In use the drill shaft is held in one hand, and the bow, the string of which goes round the shaft, is held and worked with backwards and forwards movements of the other hand.

Brace and Bit Known by such names as the brace and piercer, brace and drill, this is another hole-boring tool. It has an advantage over the auger in that it can be turned in a continuous movement. The pad is supported against the chest, and the brace is turned. The drills or spoon shaped bits are interchangable.

Bruzzer, Buzz, or Bruzz This is a heavy, sometimes all-metal 'V' shaped chisel, which is used to clean out the corners of mortises.

Calipers A pair of calipers looks rather like two slightly curved legs which are pivoted at one end. In use they can be open to set distance, and then used for measurement transference.

Chisels A chisel is a hand held cutting tool which is either held in one hand and pushed with the other, or held in one hand and banged with a mallet. The main characteristic of the carver's chisel, is that whatever special shape the cutting edge, the blade is always flat in section. The handles are usually turned in many designs and wood types, this makes for easy identification. Chisels have such names as, dog leg, fish tail, side chisel and they are usually direct descriptions of the shape of the chisel.

Compass The compass is very much like the calipers, the main difference being that on the end of one of the legs there is a socket for a pencil. The older compasses were simply dividers, and the curves were scratched rather than drawn.

Dog Irons, or Dog Stops Small shaped stops which fit into holes in the bench surface, and are used to stop the wood that is being worked from sliding forward.

Draw Knife A metal knife which has a handle at each end. In use it is held in both hands, and drawn along the wood that is being cut, towards the user. The blades are sometimes shaped, convex or concave.

Gouges The gouge is the main tool of the wood carver. It comes in a great variety of shapes and sizes, shaped and designed for specific tasks. It is used in the same way as the chisel, but usually with a lighter hand and greater care, and is primarily a shaping tool.

Gouges are known by names which describe their function, their shape, or their country of origin – outside knife, hooking knife, front bent, bent parting tool, straight maccaroni, fluteroni, etc.

Holdfasts Primarily used to hold wood fast while it is being worked, holdfasts is the group name which refers to clamps, cramps, bench screws, and a great variety of other patent wood gripping devices.

Knives Knives come in all shapes, sizes and designs, you can use any shape that takes your fancy. Many carvers grind down existing knives until they have some specific angle or bevel.

Levels One type of level is a metal plumb or ball which is suspended on the end of a string, and used for measuring vertical correctness. The other type comes in many designs. The earliest was a flat piece of wood with a ball in a groove. On a level surface the ball remained still, but when the wood was placed on a slope the ball rolled to the end of the groove.

Mallet Mallets are usually round in shape, but often ethnic carvers use mallets that are many sided. Usually made from a heavy wood such as lignum vitae, they can weigh anything up to a couple of pounds. A mallet is used when it is necessary to remove large areas of waste wood.

Planes Basically the plane is a cutting tool which is used for smoothing large flat surfaces. In design even the very early ones found at Pompeii are of a pattern that we would be able to recognise. Although there are many designs and sizes, most planes are boat shaped, and hold a blade which is at an angle to the wood that is being cut.

In use the plane is held and guided with one hand, and pushed along the surface of the wood with the other. If the blade is well set and sharp, the plane is an efficient way of removing thin shavings of wood. It has been suggested that the plane is a logical development of the small single-handed 'push adze'.

Plough and Moulding Planes Having more or less the same characteristics as the smoothing plane, the plough is a plane which is designed to remove grooves and steps. Moulding planes were used by the late medieval, linen fold panel makers. The stock and blade were shaped so that hollows and rounds of a specific pattern could be cut. The carvers and wood workers of the seventeenth, eighteenth, and nineteenth centuries used many different types of moulding planes; it was quite common to use two or three dozen different planes on one piece of work.

Punch Rather like a small cold chisel, the punch is an all-metal tool. The end that does the punching can be in a variety of patterns, but the most common is that which leaves a dotted textured surface.

Rasps and Rifflers These are group names which are given to files, or smoothers. Their main function is the removal of wood in difficult corners and hollows. Of the many types, the spoon-shaped riffler is one of the most useful.

Saws Saws were used by the Egyptians, the Romans, and most other classical wood working societies. In design they remained almost unchanged up until the seventeenth century, by which time the efficient bow and frame saws were in common use. For the carver the most useful saws are the bow, the fret, and the tenon.

Shaping Tool The modern tools of this type are known by a variety of trade names, the better ones having open, self-clearing, easily interchangable blades. Tools of this type are super efficient, and so have to be used with great care.

Slips, Stones Shaped stones which are used for sharpening chisels and gouges, made of natural or artificial stone. They are sold under many trade names, but they are commonly referred to as Washita, Arkansas, and Cone stones.

Vice A vice is an essential piece of equipment. Once again there are many designs and patterns, but the engineer's swivel vice is the most flexible and useful.

BIBLIOGRAPHY

ANDERSON, M. D. *Misericords* Penguin, 1956.

BARBEAU, MARIUS *Totem poles of the Gitksan, Upper Skeena River, B. C.* National Museum of Canada, 1973.

BOAS, FRANZ *Primitive Art* Dover, 1955.

BROUGH, J. C. S. *Timber for Woodwork* Evans, 1947.

DAY, L. F. *Ornament and its Application* Batsford, 1904.

d'AZEVEDO, WARREN L. *The Traditional Artist in African Societies* Indiana Press, 1973

FASTNEDGE, R. *English Furniture Styles from 1500–1830* Herbert Jenkins, 1962.

GARFIELD, VIOLA E. *The Tsimshian Indians and Their Arts* University of Washington, 1950.

GLAZIER, R. *A Manual of Historic Ornament* Batsford, 1906.

JACK, G. *Wood Carving, Design and Workmanship* J. Wogg, 1903.

MERCER, ERIC *Furniture 700–1700* Weidenfeld & Nicolson, 1969.

OPRESCU, G. *Peasant Art in Roumania* Studio, 1929.

SMITH, D. *Old Furniture and Woodwork* Batsford, 1949.

TOLLER, J. *Treen and other Turned Woodware* David & Charles, 1975.

153

ACKNOWLEDGEMENTS

We would like to thank all those people who let us take photographs: the staff of Nottingham Castle Museum, the Curator of Rutland County Museum, the staff of Belton House, Lincolnshire, Squire De Lisle, Quenby Hall, Leicestershire, Jack Hazelwood the carver, and others too numerous to mention.

A special thanks to Mrs E. M. Bridgewater for her financial help, and to Peter Bridgewater of Bridgewater & Grain, for his help with reproduction.

INDEX

Numbers in *italics* refer to illustrations

Adam, Robert, 99, *99*, 102
Adze, 9, *10*, *13*, 25, 26, 27, 34, 35, 36, *36*,
    41, 43, *43*, 45, 52, *57*, 115, 148, 150, 151
Alaska, 36
Alaskan hemlock, 23
Angels, carved, *28*, 66, 82, 85
Animals, carved, 122, 134
Annual rings, 21, 22
Armchair, Norwegian, *78*
Arkansas, 152
Armature, *91*
Art Nouveau panel, *18*
Ash, 23, 138
Asia, 25
Astral Islands, Oceania, *51*
Auger, 150
Australian oak, 142
Axe, 9, 35, 38, 41, 42, 150

Backgammon board, inlaid Tunbridge, *145*
Baga, 'carved-wood conscious' tribe, 47
    fertility mask, *25*
Band, 34
Barbaretti, A., *98*
Barili, Antonio, *28*, 98
Basongye mask, *47*
Bed, 73, 105, *106*, *110*, *111*, 112, 114
Bedposts, *110*
Beech, 23
Belton House, Lincolnshire, *83*, *84*, *86*, *88*, *94*
Bench, 9, 12, *12*, 14, 45, 60, 65, 66, 70, 73,
    80, 104, 114, 116, 130, 131
Bench-end, *63*, *66*, *68*
Bench screw, *13*
Berkeley Castle, *106*
Bevel, 150, 151
Birch, 138
Birds, 82
Birds-eye maple, 138
Bishop (chessman), 138
Blackthorn, 123, 127

'Bobbin chair', *109*
Bohemian cabinet, 17th century, *130*
Boulle, André and Pierre, *133*, 134, *135*
Bow drill, 150
Bow lathe, 105, *107*, 120
Bow saw, *10*, 115, *116*, 152
Bowl, 24, 38, 45, 52, 105, *118*, 120, 122, 148
Boxes, 23, 24, 38, *39*, 52, *118*, 128, 129, 131,
    134, 142
Boxwood, 23, 93, 104
Brace and bit, 150
Bruzz, 150
Bruzzer, 150
Buckinghamshire, 114
Built-up work, *28*, 29, 84, 90, 91, *92*, 112
Burghley House, *85*
Busks, *125*
Butter fats, 127
Butter markers, 120, 122, *124*
Butter mould, *32*
Burr, 16, 24
Buzz, 150

Cabinet, *130*, *135*, 144
Cabinet leg, *95*
Cabinet Maker and Upholsterer's Drawing
    Book, The, 102, *102*
Cabinet Maker and Upholsterer's Guide,
    The, 99, *100*
Cabriole legs, *95*
Calipers, 150, 151
Cambium cells, *19*
Canadian birch, 138
    red cedar, 23
Canopy bed, *110*
Carpenter, Edmund, *86*, *88*
Carpenter's tools, 12
Carvers, ethnic, 27, 127, 147, 148
Carvings
    African, 25, *25*, 26, 35, 45, *46*, 47, *47*, *48*,
        49, *50*, 52, 93, 148

American, 25, 35, 36, *36*, *37*, 38, *38*, *39*, *40*, *41*, 123, 129
English, 26, 45, 148
European, 25, 26, 35, 45, *46*
Gilded, 89
Gothic, 82, 104
Maori, *27*, *35*, *54*
Medieval, *28*, 35, 45, 66, 70, *72*, *73*, 147
Naturalistic, 29, 82, 148
Oceanic, *44*, *51*, *52*, *53*, *54*, *55*, *57*, *128*
Relief, 53, 80, *81*, 90, 138
Casket, Egyptian ebony, *128*
Castle (chessman), 138
Cedar, 23, 38, 41, 93, 123
Cells, tree, *19*, 22
Chair industry, 114, 115
Chair legs, *95*, *96*, *100*
Chairs, *30*, 31, 70, *78*, *79*, *94*, *95*, *96*, *97*, 99, *100*, *101*, 102, *102*, 105, 114, *114*, 115, *115*, 131
Charles II, 83, 84, *84*, *87*
Cherub, part of a group, *88*
Cherubim, carved, *87*
Chess, 23, *137*, 138, *139*, *140*, *141*, *142*
Chest, 45, 70, *74*, 75, *75*, *76*, 129, 131, 134
Chestnut, 23
Chip carving, 25, 35, 44, *44*, 45, 47, *52*, 53, *53*, 55, *55*, *56*, *57*, *122*, 123, *123*, *124*, *125*
Chippendale, Thomas, 93, *96*, *97*, 99, 102
Chisel, 9, *10*, *13*, 14, *16*, *17*, 29, 31, 34, 44, 47, 53, 55, *56*, 60, 65, 66, 70, 105, 130, 132, 138, 150, 151, 152
Chisel gouge, 19, 60, 79
Church, 24, 27, 63, 65, 80
Clamp, *10*, 14, 19, 55, 80, 93, 104, 112, 138, 151
Clan crest, 38
Clay, 93
Club, chip-carved, *52*, *53*, *55*
Coffins, 128
Cold chisel, 152
Columbia pine, 23
Compass, 115, 151
Congo, *47*
Cooper, 120, 122
Coping saw, *10*, *17*, 34, 70, 104, 115, *116*, 130, 138
Corset, 120, 123
Corset rods, *125*
Cosimo panel, detail of, *87*
Cosimo III, Grand Duke of Tuscany, *87*
Cosmetics casket, Egyptian, *128*
Cottage chair, 114, *114*
Cradle, supporting, *41*
Craft knife, *33*, 104
Cup, chip-carved, *123*
  turned, *118*

Cup shakes, *21*
Cupboard, 31, 134
Cutter's donkey, 136

Dapple figure, 138
Distaff, chip-carved, *122*
Dividers, *10*
Dog iron, 151
Dog-leg chisel, 151
Dog stop, 151
Dogons, 'carved-wood conscious' tribe, 47
Door post, carved, *35*, *51*, *72*, *73*
Doors, 29, 45, 55, *57*
Draw knife, *10*, 115, *116*
Drawing, carving and, 147, 149
Dresser, oak, *77*
Drift wood, 127
Drilled work, 29, 82
Drills, 9, 12, 60, 104, 116, 150
Dry wheel, 14

Ebony, 23, 92, 122, 123, *128*, 134, 138
Egg cup, 32, 120, 122, *127*
Elm, 24, 60, 115
Engineer's vice, 12, 152
England, social change in, 58
English oak, 142
Europe
  marquetry in, 134
  pre-medieval carving, 25
  social change, 58
Evelyn, John, 83
Eye motifs, *39*

Fiddle back, 138
Figure pattern, 22
Figuring, 23, 138
Fiji, *52*
Files, 9, 44
Finish, 89
Fish, carved and inlaid, *128*
Fish-tail chisel, 151
Flat chisel, *10*, 14, 27, 58
Flexible saws, 104
Floor cradle, horizontal, *41*
Floral motif, detail of, *133*
Florence, 99
Flowers, carved, *84*
Foliage, *28*, 29, 63, 75
Fork, carved, *125*
Form, the shape and character of carving, 148-9
Four-poster bed, 108, *110*
France
  linenfold panels originated in, 70
  marquetry, 134
Fret saw, 115, 130, 152

Fruit, carved, 82, *84*
Furniture, 29, *30*, 31, 34, *78*, *79*, 93, *94*, *95*, 108, 112, *112*, 115, *115*, 123, 128, *130*, 131, *134*, *144*, 145

Gentlemen and Cabinet-Makers Directory, The, 93
Germany, 136
Gibbons, Grinling, 24, 31, 82, *82*, 84, *84*, 85, *85*, *87*, 89, 91
'Gibbons peapod', *86*
Gillow, Robert, 99
Glass paper, 136
Glass scraper, 12
Glue, 82, 84, 91, 93, 112, 122, 130, 132, 136, 138, 142, 144, 145
Glue pot, *10*
Gothic
    carvers, 82, 104
    English, 83
    misericords, 90
    motifs, 73
    patterns, 99
    period, 80
Gouge, 9, *10*, *13*, 14, *14*, *15*, 16, *16*, *17*, 19, 29, 31, 45, 55, 60, 65, 66, 70, 79, 89, 104, 105, 116, 120, 130, 132, 151
Grain, of wood, 20, 22, 23, 51, 70, 78, 80, 85, 93, 104, 112, 116, 127, 132, 136, 142, 144, 148
Grease, 19, 127
Grease bowl, *38*
Green wood, 123
Grindstone, 14
Growth, yearly, 21
Guinea, *25*

Haida Indians, *37*, *40*, 41
Hand-holds, *58*, *66*, *67*, *68*
Hard wood, 14, 21, 23
'Heart' shakes, 22
Heartwood, 21, *21*, 22, 23
Hemlock, 23
    Alaskan, 23
Hepplewhite, George, 99, *100*
Hickory, 24
High Wycombe, 114
Holdfast, *12*, 14, 150, 151
Holland, 83
Holly, 24
Hooking knife, *10*, 151
Horse, 115
Hound, carving subject, *69*
House post, carved, *37*
Houses, medieval, 108

Ijo funerary screen, *48*

India, 26, 93
Indian teak, 24
Indians, American, 36, *36*, *37*, 38, *38*, *39*, *40*, 41
Industry, chair, 114, 115
Ink pots, 120
Inlaid ware, English, 142
Inlay, 32, 128, *128*, 129, *129*, 130, 131, *131*, 132, *132*, 134, 142
Intarsia, *129*
Interiors, Georgian, 24
Iroko, 24
Italian inlay, 129
Ivory, 128, *128*, *129*

Jacobean furniture, 80, *106*

Kiln-dried, 22
King (chessman), 138
'King John's Palace', Nottingham, *72*, *73*
Kitchen ware, 105, *118*, 122
Kneller, Sir Godfrey, *83*
Knife, 9, *10*, 25, 26, 27, 35, 41, 45, 47, 52, 53, 105, 123, 126, 136, 138, 151
Knight (chessman), 138
Knots, wood, 20, *21*, 22, 70, 78, 85, 123, 144
Kwakiutl Indians, 41

La Croix, Rodger, *134*
Lace cravat, carved, *84*
Lathe, 105, *106*, *107*, *108*, 114, 115, 120, 138
Legs, of chairs, *95*, *96*, *100*
Lignum vitae, 9, 24, 122, 151
Lime, 24, 80, 84, 85, 93, 104
Lincoln Cathedral, *28*, *68*
Linenfold, 70, *71*, *74*, 78, 80, *80*, 151
Linseed oil, 127
Lintel, carved, *35*, *54*
Love tokens, *31*, 32, 123

Mahogany, 24, 93, *95*,.*101*, 104, 123, 138, 144
Maine, Jonathan, *82*
Malaysia, 52
Mallet, 9, *10*, *17*, 19, 29, 34, 60, 151
Marquetry, 32, 128, 129, 132, *133*, 134, 136, 138
Masking tape, 104
Masks, 26, 38, *40*, *47*, *49*, 75, 148
Medullary rays, 22
Milking stool, Welsh, 115-16, *116*, *117*
Misericords, *28*, 58, *59*, *60*, *61*, *62*, 70, 90, 147
Mo Telemark, Norway, *46*
Model, scaled-down, *91*
Mother of pearl, 129
Moulding planes, 34, 70, 78, 151

Mouldings, 34, *89, 90*
Mouse trap, *120,* 122
Museums, 122

New Caledonia, *51*
New Zealand, *27, 35*
Nigeria, *46*
Nimba, *25*
'Nonesuch' chest, *129*
Nut crackers, chip-carved, *122*

Oak, 22, 24, 60, 62, 63, 70, 80, 104, 115, 142
Oceania, 25, 26, 45, *51,* 52
Oil, 70, 127
Oil stone, *10,* 14, 16, 19
Outside knife, 151
Overmantle, carved, *85*

Paddle, chip-carved, *50, 51*
Padouk, Indian, 142
Panelling, 34, 70, *71,* 134
Paper knife, wooden, *126*
Parana pine, 23, 144
Pastry roller, 122, *124*
Patch box, 120
Patina, 127
Patterns, 9, 22, 34
  drilled, 93
Pawn (chessman), 138
Pear, 24, 93
Pegged-work, 90, 91
Pendulum, 150
Pepys, Samuel, 83
Perspective, 149
Pew-ends, *58, 63, 64, 66, 67, 68, 69*
  Dutch, *64*
Phloem, *19*
Picture frames, 104, 142
Pierced-work, 29, 82, 93, *97*
Pillar, 108, 112
Pine, 22, 41, 80, 112, 123
Pith, 22
Planes, 9, 12, 105, 132, 151
Plinth, 108, 112
Plough, 151
Ply, 112, 138
Pole lathe, 105, *106,* 115, 120
Poles, bulbous, 108
Polish, 105, 145
Polishing, *46,* 136, 138
'Poppets', 105
'Poppy' Motif, *68*
Post box, octagonal, *121*
Pulpits, 58
Punch, *33,* 138, 152
'Puppets', 105
PVA glue, 93, 130, 132, 139, 145

Queen (chessman), 138
Quenby Hall, Leicestershire, *31, 76, 106, 111*

Rasp, 9, *9, 10, 17,* 36, *116,* 152
Red cedar, 23
Red pine, 23
Relief, carving in, 53, 80, *81,* 90, 138
Renaissance, the, 29, 34, 70, 75, 82, 91
Riffler, 9, 152
Ring shakes, 21
Romania, *122, 123*
Rome, 99
Rose wood, 24, 93, 142
Roses, *45, 65, 76*
Round gouge, 27, 58
Round shakes, *21*
Russian oak, 142

Saddle, 115
St Joseph, the carpenter, *8*
St Mary Magdalene, Newark, *60, 62, 67*
St Paul's Cathedral, *82*
Salt pots, 120
Samoa, *53*
Sand paper, *10,* 12, 36, 44, 70, 105, 126, 127,
  131, 138, 148
Sap wood, 21, 23
Sapele, 24
Satin wood, 102
Saws, 9, *10,* 12, *17,* 70, 104, 120, 152
Scandinavia, 26, 45
Scraper, 9, 44
Screen, *48,* 58, *103,* 104
Seals (letter), 120
Seasoning, wood, 22
Secretaire, rosewood-veneered, *134*
Set square, 138
Sewing-thread holder, *119*
Shakes, 21-2, *21*
Shaped slips, *15*
Shaping tools, 9, *10,* 14, *17,* 152
Shell garland, carved, *87*
Sheraton, Thomas, 102, *102*
Shrinkage, 22
Sibiiu, Romania, *122*
Siena, *98*
Sketch book, 34, 84, 149
Slips, *10,* 14, 16, 152
Snuff box, *118,* 120, 122
Soft wood, 14, 21, 23
Solomon Islands, *128*
Songye wooden mask, *49*
Spice jar, *118*
Spill vase, *118*
Spiral motifs, *54*
Spokeshave, *10*
Splat, chair, *96, 100, 114,* 115

Spoon, 9, 24, *31*, 32, *118*, 122, 123, *124, 125,*
    150, 152
Spring growth, 22
Square motif, *56*
Statue, Dengese, *47*
Star shakes, *20,* 21
Stencil, *33,* 34, *103,* 104
Sticky tape, 136, 145
Stone, 27, 84, 150, 152
Stool, 105, 114, *116, 117,* 120
    legs, *100, 116*
Straight gouge, 9
Strapwork, *76, 97*
'Supporters', 62
Swags, *82, 95, 100,* 134
Sycamore, 24, 142

Table leg, *95, 112*
Tables, 12, 45, 70, 73, *99,* 105, *111,* 142
Tea caddies, 114
Teak, 24
Techniques, Egyptian and Greek decorative,
    128
Templates, 41
Tenon saw, 70, 152
Texture, a result of sympathetic use of tools,
    148
Tiki, *51*
Tlingit Indians, 41
Tobacco jars, 114
Tomlinson's Cyclopaedia of Useful Arts and
    Manufactures Vol II, 107
Tonga, 55
Tools, 9, *10, 11,* 14, 19, *27,* 123
Tortoise-shell, 129
Totem pole, 26, *36, 37,* 38, *41, 42*
Toys, 32, 120, 122, 142
Tracing paper, 34, 136
Transylvania, *122, 124*
Treadle lathe, 31, 105, *107*
Tree, structure of, *19,* 20, 21
Treen, 23, 24, 31, 105, 120, *121,* 122, 148
Triangle motif, *53*
Trinity College, Oxford, *87*
Trundle bed, 108

Tsimshian Indians, *40*
Tudor love tokens, 123
Tunbridge ware, 32, 128, 142, *143, 144, 145,*
    146
Turned work, 23, 31, *31,* 105, *106, 108, 109,*
    112, *113,* 115, *119,* 120, *120,* 122, 138, 144
Twist, in the grain, 20
Twist drill, *36*

Undercut, carving technique, 41, 65, 84, 90-
    91, *91*

Veneers, 55, 80, 134, *134,* 136, 138
Venetian inlay, 129
Venice, 99
Vice, *10, 17,* 70, 152

Walking stick, 23, 127
Walnut, 24, 115, 142
Walpole, Horace, *84*
Washing beater, 122
Washita stone, 152
Wassail bowl, *118*
Water paint, 43, 104
Wax, 23, 70, 105, 127, 131, 136, 138, 145
Weapons, 45
Wedges, 116
West Indies, 93
'Whatnot', Victorian, 32
Wheel, 105, 115, 150
Whittling, *126,* 127, 138
William and Mary, 84
Winchester Cathedral, *68*
Windsor Castle, *82*
Windsor chairs, 114, *114,* 115
Wood workers, Egyptian, 150, 152
Woods, exotic, 123, 127, 129, 134

Xylem, *19*

Yellow cedar, 39
Yew, 23, *39,* 93, *122*
Yoruba tribe, carver from, *46*

Zaire, *49*